THE LIFE AND ART OF ATHOS MENABONI

THE LIFE AND ART OF
Athos Menaboni

Barbara Cable Taylor

MERCER UNIVERSITY PRESS
2000

ISBN 0-86554-712-2
MUP/H528

First edition.

Book designed by Mary Frances Burt.

∞The paper used in this publication meets the minimum requirements
of American National Standard for Information Sciences—Permanence of Paper
for Printed Library Materials, ANSI Z39.48-1984.

Masonite® is a registered trademark.

Library of Congress Cataloging-in-Publication Data

Taylor, Barbara Cable.
The Life and Art of Athos Menaboni / by Barbara Cable Taylor
p.cm.
Includes bibliographical references and index.
ISBN 0-86554-712-2 (alk. paper)
1. Menaboni, Athos, 1895-1990. 2. Painters—United States—Biography. I. Title.
ND237.M423 T39 2000
759.13—dc21
[B]
00-056111

Dedicated to my husband Ron,
who first introduced me to the art of Athos Menaboni,
and to our daughters Kathryn and Anne.

Acknowledgments

My sincerest appreciation to the following for granting me permission to reproduce their original Menaboni works of art in this book:

Mr. and Mrs. Dave Knoke (*Quail, Night Heron with Spanish Moss, Northern Bobwhite, Indigo Bunting, No. 95, Ruffed Grouse, Cardinal with Maple Leaves, Field Sparrow, Eastern Cardinal, Catbird*)

Mr. and Mrs. Ronald K. Taylor (*Evening Grosbeak with Blue-berried Dogwood, An Afternoon by the Fountain, Scarlet Tanager with Magnolia Leaves, Magnolia*)

D. Russell Clayton (*Serenity, La Torre del Marzocco, Becolini*)

Dr. and Mrs. Tom Cooper (*Bluebirds*)

Dr. and Mrs. John W. Bruce (*Bobwhite, colinus virginianus, Mourning Dove, zanaidura macroura*)

General and Mrs. James C. Grizzard (*Bicentennial Bald Eagle, Whooping Crane*)

Mr. and Mrs. Vernon Skiles (*Mourning Doves, Easter Robin, Red-eyed Towhee, Red-headed Woodpecker, Blue Jay, No. 40A, Wood Thrush, Eastern Bluebird,* and *Mockingbird and Catbird with Brown Thrasher*)

Mr. and Mrs. William C. Dixon, (*Cardinals*)

Doris O. Wall (*Red Camellia, Cardinals in Magnolia, White-tailed Kite*)

Saint Joseph's Health System (*Archangel*)

Tony Aeck (*Two Boys Opening the Gate, Covered Archway, Meadowlark, Florida Gallinule, Mallards, Snowy Egrets, Bufflehead*)

High Museum of Art (*Wild Turkey, Wood Duck, Brown Leghorn*)

Callaway Gardens (*Blue Jays and Snake, Prunifolia Azalea, Christmas Greenery, Mallards in Flight*)

Anonymous (*Brown Thrasher and Cherokee Rose*)

John V. Jones and John A. Chambers (*Mourning Doves on Nakora wood*)

Southern Center for International Studies (photograph of the domed breakfast room)

All photography in this book was done by George A. Clark, Marietta, Georgia with the exception of: *Wood Duck, Brown Leghorn*—photography by Peter Harholdt for the High Museum of Art; *Blue Jays and Snake, Prunifolia Azalea, Christmas Greenery, Mallards in Flight, Mourning Doves on Nakora Wood, Wild Turkey*—photography by Lee Cathey/Multi Image Studio, Inc. La Grange, Georgia

Special Thanks

A special thanks to the following people for sharing their knowledge,
Menaboni memories, and artwork with me:

Molly W. Aeck
Michael Alexander
Dr. and Mrs. M. Daniel Byrd
Mr. and Mrs. Howard H. Callaway
D. Russell Clayton
Michael Collins
Rose Cunningham
Amy Geer
General and Mrs. James C. Grizzard
Gigi Grizzard
Governor and Mrs. Joe Frank Harris
Casey Hawley
Laura Jennings
Mr. Joseph W. Jones
Dave and Chris Knoke
Tina Menaboni
Mr. and Mrs. John R. Ridley
Dr. S. A. Roddenbery
Mr. Ben Sims
Sister Michelle Carroll and Saint Joseph's Health System, Inc.
Mrs. Vernon Skiles
Paul Sternberg

The publication of this book
is made possible through a generous gift from
Tom Watson Brown of Marietta, Georgia.

Table of Contents

Athos with his pipe, 1945

Introduction

ATHOS MENABONI IS WIDELY REGARDED AS ONE of the world's finest illustrators and painters of bird life and hailed by wildlife lovers, art collectors, and ornithologists alike as the twentieth-century Audubon. A significant figure in Atlanta art, Athos Menaboni built a monumental reputation, achieving nationwide fame in the 1940s and 1950s. Like Audubon, Menaboni's attentiveness to nature is both dramatic and enchanting. His art is widespread, appearing in major museums and private homes throughout the world. His artistic talent has been an inspiration to many.

Spanning a career lasting over sixty years, Menaboni's work professed his love for the more than 150 American birds he painted in their native surroundings. Working predominantly from live bird studies, his delightful interpretations, rendered with integrity and love, capture the wondrous colors and details of nature. Through his intricate and meticulous analysis, one almost feels the artist's intimacy with the subjects he knew best—his beloved birds. His paintings offer the viewer more than just a glimpse into the wonders of the wild—he brings us closer to our fellow creatures. The artist himself said, "You cannot improve on nature, you must capture it—and transfer it to canvas."[1]

Throughout his flourishing career, his technical innovations evolved and developed. Menaboni devoted himself to experimentation, exploring a wide range of mediums: painting on canvas, silk, glass, Masonite, wood panels, gesso-covered board, mirrors. He employed tiles, eggshells, watercolors, Italian glass, and pencil. He developed the "undercoat method," a technique of painting in thin, delicate layers of oil that gives the translucency of watercolor, but allows more depth and detail than watercolor produces. Reflected in many of his works is his deep love of the sea, and his landscapes, botanicals, fantasies, and mosaics are as impressive as his birds, but it is his birds for which he is world renowned.

Menaboni was an artist for art's sake. He did not seek notoriety, instead choosing a simple, and somewhat reclusive life, content to paint what he knew and loved best. By shunning the fame and recognition he deserved, he has left the world to wonder: Who was Athos Menaboni?

The Early Years

ATHOS RODOLFO GIORGIO ALESSANDRO MENABONI was born October 20, 1895, in the Mediterranean seaport city of Livorno, formerly Leghorn—in the province of Tuscany, Italy. He was the second of five children, the eldest son, born to Jenny and Averado Menaboni. Athos (pronounced Ah'—tos) was named for the "noble Athos," the hero in Alexandre Dumas's 1844 novel *The Three Musketeers*, the book his father had finished reading just before his son's birth. Athos, his sisters Margherita and Tina, and his brother Bruno were born into a prosperous family and lived a charmed life by the sea. Life would have been idyllic had it not been for the sadness surrounding the death of Otto, the fourth of five Menaboni children. Stricken as an infant with an illness no doctor could diagnose, he died at the age of eleven.

Athos's father Averado (nicknamed Babbo) was quite accomplished in many fields. As a successful ship chandler he ran a thriving business and became a 33rd degree Mason. The Menaboni family enjoyed the good life as a result of Averado's success. Every summer they rented mountain villas for extended vacations and enjoyed extravagant parties throughout the year. Averado purchased the first automobile in town from Italian musician Giacomo Puccini, and also owned a luxury boat. Always an innovator, Averado opened a sculpture gallery as well as a movie theater in their hometown.

Babbo taught his children all he knew about nature, instilling in Athos an interest and love of wildlife very early in his life. Babbo took the children fishing, hiking, mountain climbing, and boating. While hunting with his sons, he taught them gun safety, respect for firearms, and how to be accurate marksmen. Most importantly, he instructed them in the art of good sportsmanship. Babbo was devoted to animals and often used his children as an excuse to bring animals home. Over the years, the family pets included many dogs, birds, a monkey, a mongoose, and even a Siberian wolf.

It was always the birds that held a special fascination for Athos. As a young boy, Athos spent hours in the forest watching the birds and listening to their calls. When he was only four years old, he saved his pennies and bought himself a special pet, a female sparrow, at a market. For earning good marks in school, his parents rewarded him by adding a bird each time to his burgeoning collection. His parents threatened, however, to free his birds if his schoolwork suffered. If he failed an exam at school, his father would set his birds free and he would have to start his collection over again.

In their garden, his father constructed a small aviary to accommodate his son's growing flock. Although at times Athos had fifty or more birds, his first sparrow remained his favorite and lived with him for the next eleven years until dying of old age. His love of birds continued to flourish, and eventually led to his lifetime career devoted to studying and painting birds. Birds became his obsession—a lifetime love.

Athos's Early Interest in Art

BORN WITH A LOVE AND INTEREST IN NATURE, Athos Menaboni's prolific career began as an observant child. He painted what he saw in nature, showing an aptitude for art at an early age. His first painting was a marine scene depicting his view looking out at the sea from his home. His parents appreciated his amateur talents and were a constant source of encouragement for Athos. They arranged for him to study privately, at the age of nine, under Ugo Manaresi, a famous marine painter. Manaseri told Babbo that if Athos showed promise he would train him at no charge, but added that no amount of money would be enough to teach him if Athos had no potential. Born with the eye of an artist, Athos indeed had potential. Two years later, he studied under Charles Doudelet, a well-known and highly-regarded Belgian mural painter, and served as his apprentice for three years. Soon after, he studied under Pietro Gori, a sculptor. Recognizing Athos's promising talent and ambition, Babbo and Jenny sent their teenage son to study at the Royal Academy of Art in Florence, Italy. These early lessons were never forgotten.

When World War I broke out, Athos left the Royal Academy of Art to follow in the footsteps of his father and grandfather by volunteering in the Italian army. He first served in the Signal Corps and then the Bersigliera Regiment, also known as the Sharpshooters. His father had served in the same regiment during the war in Africa, fighting against the Austro-Hungarian Empire and Germany. His grandfather, Allesandro Neri, had been one of Garibaldi's captains in the war for freedom against Austria.

For three years, Athos served in active battle. The fourth year he was an aviator flying in some of aviation's earliest aircraft. After only one month of aviation training, he piloted a reconnaissance mission along the coastal region of the Adriatic Sea in search of submarines and mines. During one mission his plane crashed on a beach, but he was lucky enough to walk away unharmed. For deactivating floating mines while swimming alongside them in the sea, he was awarded the Italian Cross of Valor for "bravery beyond the call of duty."

After the war, Italy was in a chaotic state. The Soviet government sent its agents and propaganda to Italy. To combat the Bolshevist movement, Mussolini organized his Black Shirt army. Athos enrolled in it for a year, along with his sixty-three-year-old father.

Though he served well, believing it was his obligation and duty to do so for his country, harsh army life and the war had taken its toll on Athos. He was a man who knew no enemies and being told whom he was to "hate" was against everything he believed. After the war, he returned to Livorno with a broken spirit, disillusioned, embittered, and unhappy. He had lost both faith in people and interest in all that had been important to him, especially painting.

His parents feared he might have a nervous breakdown. They tried to involve him in their daily life and his father invited him to go into the family business. Although his heart was not in it, he tried to accommodate his father, but did not have an aptitude for business and loathed mathematics. Athos was miserable.

The Voyage

THROUGH HIS BUSINESS RELATIONSHIPS, BABBO had developed friendships with many people in far-away places who were frequent guests of the Menabonis when their guests' travels brought them to Livorno. One of these friends, Captain John Hashagen, an American, stayed with the family while his ship, the *Colethraps*, a United States Maritime commission vessel, was docked in Livorno. Jenny and Babbo suggested to the captain that Athos travel with him for a year or so, hoping that the changes the voyage would provide would help their son get a fresh start and renew his interests. When the captain offered Athos the opportunity to sail with him to the United States, he was thrilled, never realizing it was his parents' intervention that afforded him the opportunity. So, getting the lowest job on the ship, as the ship's wiper, Athos earned his way to the States.

After traveling to North Africa, then the Madiera Islands, Portugal, and England, he ended up in Norfolk, Virginia. Because there was no immigration quota in 1920, all immigration officials required an immigrant to have was $100 and someone to vouch for him in order to stay ashore. With the ship's captain acting as his sponsor, twenty-five-year-old Athos was given permission to stay in the United States. He was forever indebted to Captain Hashagen and always remained in touch with him.

After a trip to New York to visit friends of his family, he stayed in the city for freelance artwork. "The first thing he painted in America was a house on Staten Island."[2] Intent on pursuing an artistic career, he supported himself decorating candles, earning only twelve dollars a week. To supplement his income he painted posters and ecclesiastical art. He was very lonely, spoke little English, and struggled financially. For enjoyment and to get his fill of the animals he missed in the city, he often visited botanical gardens, the Bronx Zoo, Central Park, and the American Museum of Natural History.

Athos never grew to like the city of New York. However, it was there, through a relative of Captain Hashagen, that he was introduced to D. P. Davis, the flamboyant millionaire real estate developer of Davis Island in Tampa Bay, Florida. Davis offered Athos a job, which he gladly accepted, pleased to have an excuse to leave New York. He became the art director and interior decorator for the Mediterranean-style resort of Davis Island in 1924, during Florida's legendary land boom. He drew many of the front elevations for the homes, hotels, and apartment buildings on the eleven-mile-long waterfront that had been "pumped up from the sea." He loved Florida for its natural wonders and his deep love of the sea was reflected in many of his early works painted during his stay. His lifestyle improved and he made many friends.

When Davis Island went bankrupt in 1926, Athos left Florida and worked his way northward. When an opportunity arose at the Al Sihah Shrine Temple in Macon, Georgia, Menaboni once again found himself serving as an interior designer. His job entailed designing a ballroom to complement the structure's Moorish architecture. Soon after, in 1927, he was directed to Atlanta for some minor commission work by friends who had told him it was a good city in which to get his start. All he owned in the world fit into one steamer trunk.

Atlanta

HIS DESTINY AWAITED HIM IN ATLANTA. AFTER only a month in this new city, he met Sara Regina Arnold, a sophomore attending Shorter College in Rome, Georgia, and an Atlanta debutante, at a party. She had come to Atlanta by train (from Rome) for the weekend for dates with two different "beaus." While visiting her aunt and uncle in a boarding house they operated downtown on Peachtree Street, where Crawford W. Long Hospital is now located, she met Athos who was renting a room in the very place. She was quite taken with the fascinating foreigner. Athos was smitten, too, and saw Sara every day for a week. It was love at first sight for them, though they appeared to be complete opposites, and he proposed marriage at the end of the week.

Athos's mother in Italy had hoped he would find a nice Italian girl to marry in the United States. She was delighted when he corresponded with her to tell her he was to marry a wonderful girl from Rome. Of course, Athos neglected to mention that Sara was from Rome, Georgia, not Rome, Italy. Sara's parents were not thrilled with the prospect of their daughter, raised in the Southern Baptist tradition, marrying an artist, a Catholic one at that, with no steady income, when she had other suitors who had much more promising futures. Athos strove passionately to gain approval from Sara's parents. During a visit to Rome, Georgia, in which he was introduced to her parents, he was asked to paint a mural in their neighbor's house and Athos's approval was assured. He formally asked permission in writing to marry Sara and finally received her parents' blessing.

Sara was twenty and Athos thirty-one when they married on August 14, 1928, a year after he had proposed. They honeymooned for three months in Italy. Sara always felt that their time there was the best investment she and Athos ever made. Sara met and grew to love Athos's family during their extended honeymoon while learning all about his European homeland and his upbringing by the sea, which was so different from her own.

After the honeymoon, with only about forty dollars to their names, they returned to Atlanta, where they had deliberately chosen to make their home because they found the people warm and friendly. With no steady job, living from one painting commission to the next, their money was stretched tight. Fortunately, a friend came to visit them with a belated wedding gift of twenty dollars, and this seemingly enormous amount provided them with enough money for their first apartment, on Eleventh Street, in midtown Atlanta. A pair of canaries and a potted plant were the first purchases made by Mr. and Mrs. Athos Menaboni. As time went on, they continued to add more birds and plants to their home—a tradition that would continue for the rest of their lives.

The marriage, a true partnership and a tremendous success, produced no children. They worshipped each other and were completely devoted to one another. Together they shared their love of nature and wildlife; this bond was remarkable and unwavering.

Mr. and Mrs. Athos Menaboni

Athos

ATHOS WAS VERY OLD FASHIONED, WITH TRADITIONAL values and standards, and always a gentleman. He was very likable, mannerly, soft spoken, considerate, and kind. With his dark hair and trim mustache, he was quite a dashing Italian. He spoke with imperfect English and a thick Italian accent. Sara often filled in the correct English words for him when he spoke. Some say he had bird-like features, perhaps because he was so short and slight and his prominently long Florentine nose was crooked, evidence of it having been broken.

Athos told friends he would have been happy living on a deserted island. He hated crowds and traffic and anything he considered artificial such as dyed hair. He disliked disingenuous people, cold food, and modern music. He was not a fan of modern art, nor was he impressed by modernists and did not consider their "blobs" of paint on any medium to be art. In his opinion, true art was self-contained and should need no explanation. Most assuredly, he believed art required skill, training, practice, and experimentation. He believed the more he painted, the more he learned.

Unconcerned about being "discovered," Athos neither aspired nor attempted to become internationally acclaimed. When asked to judge others' artwork, he loathed the task, and after judging art a handful of times, he swore he would never judge another's work again. He was never comfortable at gallery exhibitions where he was to be the center of attention and he would not make public speeches or appear on television or radio. From the first, Sara always acted as Athos's representative.

Friends always felt welcome at the Menabonis' home. Athos especially enjoyed small dinner parties using plain W. J. Gordy pottery, where he could enjoy intimate conversations with good friends. He abhorred gossip. He was well versed in world politics (proud to have become a United States citizen in 1936) but avoided talking about local politics and religion. He thought big parties were a waste of time because there was never sufficient time to exchange thoughts and he did not like to mix and mingle at cocktail parties.

Always charming and thoughtful, Athos made his guests feel special, as though they were the only guests he had ever received. He made friends for life. In spite of his quiet, unassuming demeanor, friends sensed they were with greatness when they were in his presence. When guests left after a visit, Athos would always walk them to their car and remain standing until their car was out of sight down the long curving driveway.

Athos was deeply devoted to his exceptionally close-knit family and went out of his way to help them. After World War II, he brought his sisters, Tina and Margherita, and his mother, Jenny Menaboni, to the United States. Prior to their move, he had arranged for them to spend a year and a half in Cuba in order to get on the immigration quota list. (In Livorno, the Menaboni home had been leveled and all earthly possessions lost during an air raid. His father had died of natural causes during the war and his brother Bruno remained in Italy to take over the business.) Athos and Sara invited Tina, Margherita, and Mama Menaboni to temporarily reside at their small home. Meanwhile, the couple willingly took up residence in one of the aviaries located on the back of their property. Since the only kitchen was in the tiny house, the Menaboni women took turns cooking for one week at a time. Later, Athos helped them establish themselves in a house of their own in Brookhaven (a suburb of Atlanta) and remained in close contact with them. Athos's mother died ten years after coming to the United States at the age on ninety-two. She very much enjoyed her time in Atlanta with Athos and Sara.

Athos did not attend church, but was a deeply religious man in a private way. Many religious paintings were displayed in his home. He often looked out his window at nature's bounty and told friends that nature was his religion. Embellishing the Japanese-style gardens he established around his home were religious sculptures, many of which he had sculpted himself from Georgia clay and cement. A small statue of St. Francis of Assisi, patron saint of all living things, hung outside his house.

Nature filled him completely and he painted from the heart. He only needed nature's beauty, his family, and friends to feel complete. Sara wrote, "Should this man never paint another picture, he would keep busy creating beautiful objects of one kind or another. But he could not live happily without the nature wonderland he finds outside his doorstep and on his travels. And he would be a very, very lonely man were he stripped of his myriad relatives and friends."[3]

Athos always tried to accommodate Sara. When the couple were well into their eighties, a friend asked Athos how he and Sara stayed happily married for so long. Athos simply replied, "Yes dear." The friend asked what he meant by that and Athos explained that whenever Sara asked for or wanted anything he would simply say, "Yes dear." This was their secret.

Sara

Sara was sturdy, buxom, and feisty; quite a colorful character whose deep resonant voice had a slow Southern drawl. She had a heart of gold, but was strong willed, quite outspoken, often overbearing, vocal, and quick to give orders. The Menabonis in Italy nicknamed her "Il Duce," meaning "the leader," after Benito Mussolini, when she was organizing her wedding to Athos. Sara never flinched when it came to getting what she wanted accomplished. This domineering quality of hers was probably a godsend for Athos.

Though always gracious, at times Sara seemed quite austere, intimidating, and often times bombastic. The Menabonis welcomed many visitors to their home, but Sara wanted to know people before they entered her home. Guests were expected to be punctual and enter the Menaboni home with respect and appreciation for the artist whom she adored or they would not be asked back. Visits to her home had to be scheduled in advance.

A friend of the Menabonis remembered going to their home with her young daughter to have some prints signed for the Atlanta History Center. Arriving at exactly the designated time, they approached the front door. Sara was waiting for them. In her deep and intimidating voice she asked the small child if she had ever been in the home of an artist before. Naturally, the girl was in awe of the large woman and quite terrified to enter her home. Gathering up all her courage she marched into the Menaboni house. Once inside, Sara took control—she was the business manager and there were no two ways about it. By the end of the visit, however, Sara and the young girl were giggling, snacking on milk and cookies, and getting along famously.

Sara needed people. Every Sunday afternoon she hosted a gracious and much anticipated tea. Always a congenial and hospitable hostess, she invited people of all ages and professions to these teas which

Athos and Sara enjoying their role as guests of honor at the Bird Club House Party, St. Louis, Missouri

began precisely at 4:00 PM and generally lasted several hours. Often times, personalized cocktail napkins set the tone. They read: "Good Times...Good Friends...Good Cheer...Sara and Athos are glad you're here!" Usually, three couples were invited to share in this wonderful tradition and weekly get-together, which Sara and Athos enjoyed as much as their guests did. Sara was so bold that she instructed her guests how to concoct their tea, with her specific amounts of cream or sugar, and which cookies to sample and in what order. Often, Sara's ulterior motive for these teas was to interest prospective buyers in Athos's work. She and Athos cultivated many friendships during these teas and these many diverse connections kept them young at heart.

Athos often told friends that Sara was like the FBI. She loved to interrogate people. Once, the former First Lady of Georgia, Elizabeth Harris (wife of then Governor Joe Frank Harris), wanted to visit the Menabonis at home for fifteen minutes to have them sign their book, *Menaboni's Birds*, for the library of Georgian authors in the governor's mansion. Mrs. Harris' press secretary phoned Sara to see if that would be all right. Sara said "No, that would not do." The press secretary, rather taken aback, asked Sara if she was refusing a visit from the governor's wife. Sara said she was certainly not refusing the visit, but Mrs. Harris could not just stay for fifteen minutes, she must stay at least an hour, long enough so that Sara could get to know her. Elizabeth Harris did come for an extended visit and they became fast and longtime friends.

No one could contact Athos without first going through Sara. Throughout the marriage, she handled the finances and his schedule. He was the genius and did not like to be bothered with the little details. Sara acted as his agent, doing everything she could to establish Athos as a well-known artist, and pushing him to do exhibits and other events in order to popularize him and keep his work flourishing.

Her love for Athos was so intense that she wanted the world to know him. In the late 1930s, Sara sent thirty-six of Athos's paintings to her sister-in-law, Mrs. Henry B. Arnold, in New Jersey, and asked her to see if she could find anyone interested in showing his work. Within three weeks, the venture resulted in Menaboni's first major exhibition, at the American Museum of Natural History in New York. An exhibit at the Kennedy Gallery in New York followed. The National Audubon Society used these same paintings in an exhibit that traveled throughout the United States for two years.

Sara was completely protective of her beloved Athos and loved him deeply all her married life. A friend remembered visiting the Menabonis when they were well into their eighties. Athos had to excuse himself from the room for a moment. Sara looked after him as he left the room and said, "I'm just crazy about him and always have been."

St. Francis watches over Valle Ombrosa

Valle Ombrosa

AFTER APARTMENT LIVING, ATHOS AND SARA SETTLED in a rental home in Sandy Springs (north of Atlanta) and Athos immediately set about constructing an aviary in the spacious backyard. A tenderness existed between Athos and his birds—his contact with them was intimate. Birds knew no fear of him and trusted him like one of their own, often eating from his hands. "People don't think of birds as affectionate, but they are," he told others.[4]

He collected, painted, and cared for his birds while Sara busied herself writing for numerous publications and giving "bird" talks throughout the Atlanta area. Athos tried his hand at teaching art, but realized after a few months that he was actually painting for all his students. They were active in many ornithological organizations, including the National Audubon Society, as well as working with many Scout troops, nature conservation groups, garden clubs, and museums in the Southeast. They loved to travel and enjoyed extended trips every three years or so to places such as Mexico, Italy, and Japan. Athos, the pilot, always retained a love of flying. In his later years, he and a friend (who owned Dekalb Peachtree Airport) spent countless hours flying over Georgia. The Menabonis relished the simple pleasures life had to offer, frequenting museums, "birding," taking photographs, and enjoying long, frequent walks. They were always enthralled with new discoveries, whether it be sighting a new bird or plant species or uncovering a plant or home for one of nature's creatures.

They were completely content with their lives. The morning they awoke to silence—no cackling, no gaggling of geese, and no chirping—their world changed. Neighborhood dogs had broken through the wire of their aviary, killing many of their beloved birds and ducks in a hideous attack. The loss absolutely devastated Athos. Immediately, Sara's efforts to shield her husband from future distress began.

She realized that if they owned their own land, they could build the sturdiest aviaries possible without rental restrictions and limitations, and their precious birds could enjoy a safe haven. In 1939, she contacted a real estate agent who showed her a 5.5-acre piece of property in Sandy Springs, and in turn, brought Athos to see the property, which was only one mile from their rental home. The rugged, unspoiled terrain with a natural barrier formed by hills on three sides of the property, complete with a beautiful waterfall, was exactly the peaceful woodland sanctuary they had desired. They purchased the property, fourteen miles outside Atlanta, on the same afternoon they first laid eyes on it.

It was here at 1111 Cook Road, later renamed Crest Valley Drive, that Athos and Sara lived quietly and spent the remainder of their lives. The longer they stayed, the more they realized how much they loved their Atlanta home and both knew they never wanted to leave. In fact, Sara told friends that she and Athos had originally decided to give Atlanta a try for five years. After that time she said it would have taken dynamite to move them because they had grown to love the Atlanta area and its people so much. They named their property "Valle Ombrosa," meaning "shady valley" in Italian, in memory of Valle Ombrosa, a town north of Florence, Italy, where Athos had spent his boyhood summers.

Merry Christmas
Sara and Athos Menaboni

A Christmas card from the Menabonis

Cardinals, circa 1950

Two Boys Opening the Gate, dated 1928

Covered Archway, dated 1928

Serenity, dated 1928

Eastern Cardinal, No. 92, circa 1940

Archangel, dated 1928

Photograph of the domed breakfast room in the Southern Center for International Studies, circa 1930

An Afternoon by the Fountain, dated 1932

Catbird, circa 1940

Wild Turkey, circa 1940

Eastern Bluebird, No. 79 A, circa 1940

Red-eyed Towhee, circa 1940

Red-headed Woodpecker, No. 316, circa 1940

Easter Robin, circa 1940

Mathatiana, Camellia Japonica, circa 1950

Brown Thrasher and Cherokee Rose, circa 1948

Field Sparrow, No. 17 A, circa 1940

The House

ATHOS AND SARA WERE SENSIBLE, PRACTICAL, completely unpretentious, and accustomed to living frugally when money was tight. Plans for their home were finished only days before the bombing of Pearl Harbor. The actual construction had to be delayed because of insufficient funds and the outbreak of World War II. The Menabonis were not defeated, rather they believed and often boasted, "We thrive under difficulties." They asked their close friend, architect Richard L. Aeck, founder of Aeck Associates, if he could turn the proposed two-car garage into living quarters. During the first year of the war, they spent $3500 on the construction of their traditional house (the intended garage), terrace, and walls. The result was a simple brick home that measured 25 feet to a side, built on a hill, and set deep in the woods. They put the remainder of their money into ponds, a small lake, bird cages, and fencing for their bird sanctuary.

Their lifestyle was anything but extravagant, in fact, almost Bohemian. The first night in their new home, they spent entertaining friends who sat on crates (eventually replaced with

Danish-modern furniture) while they dined. The entire wall of the living room was constructed entirely of glass, bringing the outdoors in, and giving the illusion of added space. In the center of another wall was a small fireplace. Bird feeding stations were outside the big picture window and cages of birds were in front of all the windows in the small home. The dining room was charming and compact, but functional, and housed an indoor aviary filled with finches and tropical birds. At one time, a bird even sat on her eggs in a basket Athos had attached to the dining room chandelier. The indoor aviary was especially unique in that it contained a real pond, rocks, ferns, moss, and two live trees that were actually rooted in the earth—almost as though the walls and roofing for much of the small haven were placed directly on top of the earth. No doubt, this lack of flooring was one reason why many of the Menabonis' friends remembered the house being so chilly.

The kitchen resembled a ship's galley but provided Sara with all the space she needed to prepare the gourmet meals for which she was well-known. No rugs were placed on top of the tile floors that were throughout the house. Both bedrooms were somewhat odd, having small built-in cubicles for beds. The rooms resembled sleeping cars on a train. When Sara had a heart attack in her later years, the family doctor summoned to their home found Athos hovering over her in her tiny room. So limited in size was the room that the doctor turned to Athos and said that there was not enough room for both of them, and he thought he should be the one to stay. To show his gratitude for their continued good care, Athos painted their personal physician one painting each year.

The house also doubled as a bird clinic and sanctuary. A coot once occupied their shower that served as home to many recovering birds who were moved only when Athos and Sara needed to bathe. Constant chirping resonated throughout their home. Athos knew the songs and distress calls of all the birds he painted and cared for and was able to communicate with his "house guests" quite easily. Birds flew freely throughout their home; Sara and Athos were oblivious to the mess their droppings made. Their guests noticed, but never said a word. Sara wrote of retrieving a young American Kestrel (commonly known as "Sparrow Hawk") named Joseph from a woman's apartment sill.

> I told her the joys of having a sparrow hawk, and asked her why she did not herself wish to keep him free in her apartment until he was old enough to be liberated? Oh, no, Joseph was not house-broken and would streak her furniture and draperies with droppings. I brought Joseph to my own house, where he could leave his "calling cards" all over my furniture, draperies and rugs! Furnishings could be cleaned or replaced, but nothing could ever replace the fun and additional bird data we got from Joseph until we released him.[5]

The main house was never built, instead additions were eventually added to the brick structure as money permitted. The original house (the intended garage) always remained the core of their home. Sara and Athos never owned a credit card or owed money for anything. Athos had learned in the old country to pay cash for everything.

Athos constructed two aviaries on the back of the Valle Ombrosa property which at times were home to Wild Turkeys, Mallards, sparrows, hawks, crows, flickers, wild geese, pheasants, tree ducks, and others. A Golden Eagle, given to them by the San Diego Zoo where

25

it had been raised from its nest, enjoyed a peaceful existence in one of the aviaries for twelve years. Often the Menabonis would order live birds and ducks from as far away as California to grace their home or aviaries and many of these became subjects for his paintings.

He fashioned himself as a bird healer and when necessary used the aviaries as rehabilitation centers. Birds were brought to him from people all over Georgia who had heard of his talent for nursing injured birds back to health. Children often brought him birds that had tumbled out of their nests and broken a wing or fallen victim to a neighborhood cat. He always did whatever he could to help. To spare the children's feelings, he never told them if "their" bird had died. Losing a bird was heartbreaking for Athos. On occasion, he performed his own autopsies for the purpose of understanding and preventing future maladies.

Most of the property at Valle Ombrosa was left undisturbed, the way nature had intended it. Spectacular camellia bushes lined ivy-covered walkways, carefully laid and maintained by Athos, that fit perfectly amidst the woodland. He and Sara spent as much time out doors as their schedules allowed, relishing all nature had to offer. His extensive bonsai (dwarf Japanese trees) collection took over a large portion of his home and gardens.

During the war years, the sanctity and beauty of Valle Ombrosa was Athos's salvation. He worried for his family still in Italy. After hearing ominous reports of the war in Europe on the radio, Athos often left his studio to take long walks on his 5.5 acres of paradise.

He often found his source of inspiration for a painting in his own backyard. On one of his many walks, Athos found an injured Rose-breasted Grosbeak and took it home to nurse back to health. He

26

realized that keeping this particular species in a cage was illegal and sought the advice of a judge, who happened to be a friend of his. The judge sentenced Athos to care for the grosbeak for the remainder of its life and Athos happily complied with the judge's order.

Loving all animals, in addition to his birds, he nurtured many pets. One dark night while driving to a party, he accidentally struck a rabbit in the road. Having no time to give the creature a decent burial, he picked it up and put it in the trunk of his car, thinking the hawk in his aviary could feast upon it the next day. Late the next afternoon, Sara remembered the rabbit in the trunk and dreaded the stench that awaited her. With fear and trepidation, she opened the trunk and was surprised to find the bunny staring at her, alive and well, but minus his two front teeth. Knowing that the rabbit's front teeth would eventually grow back, Athos patiently fed the toothless fellow with a syringe until nature took its course. The rabbit received such kind care that when it was time to set him loose, he would not leave and he became yet another member of the beloved menagerie residing at Valle Ombrosa.

Indigo Bunting, No. 95, circa 1940

The Studio

ORIGINALLY, AN AVIARY ON A HILL OF VALLE Ombrosa served as Athos's studio. In 1962, a large, light, airy, and comfortable studio overlooking a valley was added. It was easily accessible from steps outside their kitchen. The new studio was nearly the size of the original house. Three sides of the spacious studio were paneled in Nakora wood, a rare, heavily-grained, blonde-colored wood grown in the Philippines and processed in Japan. Athos loved this wood when he first saw it on a visit to Japan and also made their dining room table from it. The fourth wall of the studio was composed entirely of glass, allowing the maximum amount of north light into the studio, and affording a view from the artist's easel directly overlooking the woods and out to the gold fish pond he had lovingly constructed. Athos never painted using artificial light. Knowing how imperative the perfect lighting conditions were for her husband's work, Sara scheduled all their meetings during the lunch hour and later tea time. In the mornings he cared for his birds, and after lunch, he painted until dark, maximizing the use of natural light his studio provided. On dark and dreary days when the lighting in his studio was unsuitable for painting, he often read travel and history books, biographies, worked on elaborate model ships, or sculpted.

Most of his art supplies were purchased at Miller's Book Store in Buckhead. At Miller's a strong bond of friendship was formed in the late 1950s with John Ridley, the store's manager. After one visit to the store Athos inadvertently left his sketchbook on the counter. John Ridley called the artist and offered to return the sketchbook to him at home. Athos was reluctant to accept the offer, not wanting to inconvenience anyone. He was assured by the manager that it would be no trouble for him. Ridley did take the sketchbook to Athos at Valle Ombrosa and the two men had an interesting and enjoyable visit that marked the beginning of a long-lasting friendship. Ridley and his wife, Mary Ella, enjoyed many Sunday teas at the Menabonis' home and were the recipients of numerous paint-

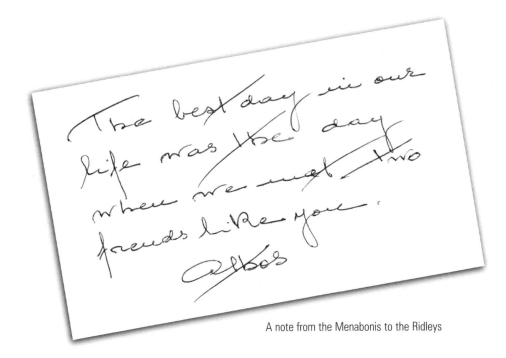

A note from the Menabonis to the Ridleys

Athos painting, circa 1950

ings done by Athos over the years. The Ridleys, in turn, donated and shared many of their Menaboni "treasures" with museums and others in later years.

Menaboni hated clutter and was as painstakingly fastidious about his studio as he was about his paintings, always keeping it impeccably neat and orderly. Every brush, paint, and solvent container had its proper place. His wooden paint box was very primitive looking, as was his enormous easel. Sliding doors on one wall of the studio concealed books and painting equipment as well as stuffed birds used for study. Cages of birds filled his studio and a screech owl often perched on his easel as he worked. Sara often read to him as he painted. His companion dog, who was very much part of the family, stayed by his side at all times. Over the years he had cockers, setters, shepherds—his favorite was Lupo, and two Italian greyhounds.

31

Saint Joseph's Infirmary, 1928. Menaboni murals flank the alter.

His Career Takes Off

Early Mural Commissions

ATHOS WAS HAPPIEST PAINTING BIRDS, BUT HIS early income was dependent on his mural works which were done in a variety of unusual mediums and in various styles. In the late 1920s, in hopes of finding employment, Athos made a portfolio of his sketches and took them to architects around Atlanta. At the firm of Hentz, Adler and Shutze, Athos met Philip Trammell Shutze, a brilliant young architect who had worked in Rome, Italy, and studied at the American Academy there for five years. Shutze spoke Italian fluently and was able to communicate well with Athos, who still spoke in Italian and fragmented English. There was a mutual respect and admiration between the two. Meeting Philip Shutze, who has been described as America's greatest classical architect, proved to be a golden opportunity for Athos, setting his career in motion.

Shutze arranged for Athos to do some decorative painting in the Edward Inman House, later known as the Swan House. Shutze had designed the house, which was completed in 1928. It was said that Emily Caroline MacDougald Inman, wife of Charles Inman, an

Atlantan whose family fortune was made primarily in the cotton business, was insistent that the hottest new artist in Atlanta paint something in her English country dream home (six miles north of their previous house in Ansley Park) which later became a house museum owned by the Atlanta Historical Society. The house was already completely finished to perfection when she invited Athos to add his famous touch in 1928. Reportedly, Mrs. Inman did not like the imported Italian pink marble in the second floor bathroom and hired Athos to paint green faux marble over the real marble walls. He also painted a series of ornamental swans on the ceiling and stars over the vanity. Athos thought the idea of painting faux on top of real marble was rather silly, but nonetheless, the finished results thoroughly delighted Mrs. Inman.

This successful venture opened many doors for Athos in Atlanta and many of the prominent families of Atlanta would commission Athos to paint for them. The most elite social circles welcomed Athos and Sara. Athos's mural works eventually brought him nationwide fame and numerous awards. His work for Emily Inman was so outstanding that soon after he finished it he was asked to recreate the same green marbled scagliola look on the columns inside the Reformed Jewish Temple (called the Temple of the Hebrew Benevolent Congregation and also designed by Shutze) on Peachtree Street.

In the late 1920s, Athos painted a continuous landscape mural in the breakfast room of Glenridge Hall, the Tudor-style mansion owned by steel industry magnate T. K. Glen, on Glenridge Drive in Sandy Springs. The vines and trees painted in his mural later deteriorated because of water damage to the home's masonry wall, requiring restoration in the late 1980s. Some sixty years after the original commission, the owner called Sara and Athos to gain information that might help in the restoration project. Sara quipped that "maintenance was not in the original contract." This was typical Sara, always wearing her business-woman's hat.

In early 1928, Menaboni was engaged to paint the sky over the war picture in Atlanta's Cyclorama, consequently completing the great canvas which was originally the work of several German artists, executed in 1886. "Painting the ceiling of the Cyclorama was like flying in an airplane," Athos recalled. "I had to stand on such high scaffolds while putting a sky above the battle scenes that I thought I was back in flying school, or in the war. When the job was finished, I had the same satisfaction I felt when I made a safe landing in a plane."[6]

The Haverty family of Atlanta commissioned him in 1928 to create two murals to be used as altar pieces for the Gothic Chapel in Saint Joseph's Infirmary in Atlanta. On separate canvases, Menaboni created two archangels, each approximately six feet tall, that were hung on either side of the altar. One angel, clothed in red, plays a trumpet while the other angel is clothed in green and plays a small pipe. The angels were removed in prepatory placement in 1978 when the new Saint Joseph's Hospital sponsored by Sisters of Mercy was built. Only one of the canvases was easily removable and hangs in the lobby of the newer Saint Joseph's Hospital. The other canvas was badly damaged by radiator heat and was deemed beyond restoration by Athos. The damaged canvas was painstakingly salvaged and preserved by Dr. S. A. Roddenbery, a brother of one of the Sisters of Mercy at Saint Joseph's Hospital. Eventually this restored archangel made its way to the first house of Mercy, the Chapel of Mercy International Centre in Dublin, Ireland, where it now hangs.

In the lobby of the classic Rhodes-Haverty Building in downtown Atlanta, Athos painted laurel wreaths and acanthus medallions in soft shades while creating a Renaissance Florentine style ceiling in 1929. After being concealed for thirty years by a false ceiling, this masterpiece was uncovered just before the artist's death in 1990, during the building's renovation by workers who spotted Menaboni's signature in a corner. Though in need of restoration, the discovery sparked much surprise and excitement and thrust Menaboni in the spotlight again. Always humble, he told friends that he did not know why people were so excited about uncovering this mural, because it was not one of his better works. Even at the age of ninety-four he could remember having a terrible headache while working on this mural because he had to lie on his back and lean upwards while painting directly on the ceiling during the entire project.

The restoration expert was left to his own devices to figure out Menaboni's palette, and was surprised to discover that Athos had used colors straight from his tube of paint in this mural and other early works. The same virgin colors had been used in painting the Swan House's swans and stars. He thinned his tube colors in his marbleizing work. As his style developed, he began mixing his palette colors; his first attempt was the mural in Glenridge Hall.

In 1930, Menaboni painted a whimsical fantasy in the octagonal domed breakfast room of the Goodrum-Abreau House, also designed by Shutze in 1928. Located at 320 West Paces Ferry Road, the home was also later known as the Peacock House and later became The Southern Center for International Studies. By painting Baroque-style trellis work with climbing grapevines and morning glories, the room looked like the inside of a bird cage. Birds are perched in the midst of his design and parrots chase after dragon-flies while Chinese figures and vases decorated with Oriental motifs accentuate the beauty of this design. It was here that birds first started appearing in Athos's mural work. After this commission, the number of birds depicted in his murals increased considerably.

About this same time, he was commissioned to paint four panels featuring the Italian countryside views in the octagonal room of the Albert Howell House. The home, designed by architect Albert Howell, had an Italian flair and rested on seven acres above Peachtree Creek in Atlanta. In November 1936, Athos painted panels and a decorative ceiling for the Henry Grady Hotel in Atlanta. These panels were adorned with pelicans and monkeys settled in greenery amidst their native surroundings. The vines entwined on the ceiling in a circular pattern formed a star-like medallion decorated with leaves and berries.

Merry Christmas
Sara and Athos Menaboni

A Christmas card from the Menabonis

The Woodruff Connection

ANOTHER INFLUENTIAL AND POWERFUL FORCE in Athos's life was Atlanta legend Robert Winship Woodruff who joined the Coca-Cola Company as president in 1923. Woodruff was introduced to Menaboni's work in the late 1930s when a few Coca-Cola executives provided funds to buy him *Doves in Long Leaf Pine* from the Kennedy Gallery in New York. The painting's vibrant qualities made such an impression on Woodruff (who admired the wild and its inhabitants as much as Menaboni) that he had a lithograph made from it and used it for his family Christmas cards in 1941. The cards were such a sensation that Woodruff commissioned Menaboni to paint one the next year (*The Bobwhite Quail*) and then again the following year. The working relationship with Woodruff continued and for forty-four years until Woodruff's death in 1985, Menaboni painted for the beautiful and eagerly-awaited cards, which the Smithsonian Institution in Washington, DC, has called the nation's finest Christmas card collection. Woodruff would often suggest the bird subjects he wished to have painted and each spring Athos would submit three or four paintings to Mr. Woodruff for his approval. His final selection would appear on the Woodruff card that year. *The Great Blue Heron* was the last lithograph to appear in the Woodruff series in 1984. Menaboni also painted or sketched many of his own personal Christmas cards as well as a card for the National Audubon Society in 1954, which featured a Cardinal and pine boughs.

Most of the original paintings from which Woodruff chose his card subjects featured game birds and song birds seen on Ichauway Plantation, the 30,000 acre farm in south Georgia owned by Woodruff. Athos painted many of these birds from memory or using stuffed birds on loan from museums, having only visited the plantation on a few occasions. His visits enabled him to capture the feel and atmosphere of Ichauway while studying the wildlife indigenous to the area. Two paintings, (*The Mountain Bluebird* and *The Western Meadow Lark)*, however, feature birds from the TE Ranch, the Woodruff's northwest Wyoming property, which Athos never had the opportunity to visit.

The Brown Thrasher and Cherokee Rose (Georgia's state bird and state flower), painted in 1948, became famous throughout the state. The painting was first lithographed and printed on Woodruff's Christmas cards that year and then reprinted on the cover of the *Atlanta Journal Magazine* in May 1949. Then Woodruff and the Atlanta Historical Society collaborated to have 6000 color reprints produced that were turned over to the Georgia Department of Education. They, in turn, distributed the prints to every school in the state. The Atlanta Historical Society issued a statement expressing their hope that the painting would inspire the study of Georgia's history and create an increasing appreciation of art. The original oil painting was given to former First Lady of Georgia, Betty Talmadge, wife of then Governor Herman Talmadge, and hung in the governor's mansion.

Many of the Christmas cards are featured in the rare book *Ichauway Plantation* (1974) by Charles Elliott. He wrote:

> Both Mr. And Mrs. Woodruff were patrons of Athos Menaboni, who is widely acclaimed as the modern Audubon. Menaboni is a master craftsman and a vivid interpreter of the outdoor world. A number of his paintings hang on the walls at Ichauway and over the years he has done some remarkable portrayals of the Plantation birds. The Woodruffs share these with their friends by sending them out each year as Christmas cards. It originally started with the game birds, but since then the list has extended through most of the song birds found along the creek and pine woods of the Plantation.[7]

In addition to the Christmas card commissions, Woodruff frequently contracted Athos to paint for the Ichauway Plantation homestead itself. One such painting mapping out the plantation was requested, as well as an unusual painting which showed the different birds of the plantation and detailed their different rates of speed. During one of his stays at Ichauway Plantation, Woodruff offered Athos a peacock for his aviary at Valle Ombrosa. The noisy peacock kept Athos up all night while conducting its mating ritual. After losing a good night's sleep, Athos kindly declined Woodruff's offer. A few paintings hung in the TE Ranch home as well. Moreover, Mr. Woodruff frequently commissioned Athos to paint other birds and botanicals for him throughout the years, and these paintings he gave to family, close friends, and neighbors as gifts.

WOOD DUCK
ICHAUWAY PLANTATION

1954 Woodruff Christmas card
Wood Duck, Ichauway Plantation, 1954

South End House

SARA AND ATHOS ENJOYED FIVE MONTHS ON Sapelo Island, Georgia, in 1938, living at South End House, the mansion of tobacco magnate Richard (R. J.) Reynolds. During their stay, Athos was commissioned to paint murals in five rooms in the mansion. Sara served as Athos's assistant in the projects, but never did any painting herself. They loved Sapelo for its abundance of bird species and in their free time busied themselves collecting information from their discoveries. Of their Sapelo Island experience Sara proclaimed, "[T]hey reveled in being in a nature paradise of fauna and flora." Athos took his camera and sketchbook to record his new bird sightings on his outings from one end of the island to the other.

The paintings in the Reynolds mansion were unique. Each room possessed its own theme, chosen by R. J. himself. A ringmaster, lions, and monkeys filled the child's room walls. Reportedly, Mrs. Reynolds hated this circus theme and while her husband was away, hired another painter to paint over completely with sky blue paint one of the walls with Menaboni's murals. Seeing this upon his return, R. J. was furious. In the game room that housed the mansion's bowling alley, a pirate theme covered the walls. Athos added a comical touch of his own by painting a lady sitting on a commode on the back of one of the doors. Throughout the home, squirrels, monkeys, and cardinals were painted perched on palm trees, greenery, and bamboo railings.

Over the years, many of the murals that had been painted on canvases and glued to the mansion walls were damaged due to heat and humidity, especially those in the room that housed the heated indoor swimming pool. A caretaker for the mansion cut many of the canvases as they began to deteriorate and detach themselves from the walls and framed them for hanging inside the mansion. Fortunately, in doing so, he unknowingly preserved many of the original colors in Menaboni's palette, making restoration possible.

More Notable Mural Works

SOON AFTER ITS COMPLETION, IN EARLY 1939, Menaboni painted the L-shaped main hall of the Patterson-Carr home in Atlanta. The early American architecture of this home, designed by Philip Shutze, resembled an eighteenth-century farm-house. By painting the entire hallway that led to an enclosed outdoor garden with native dogwood trees and butterflies, Menaboni created the image of an indoor bower.

Later the same year, with superb skill, he used an eighteenth-century technique of reverse painting on glass when creating murals in the windowless dining room of the Mirador Room in the Capital City Club in downtown Atlanta. Fifteen mirrored panels were conceived and executed by Athos in this backward process where the final touches were painted first. Athos used his mural treatment, featuring the flora and fauna of Atlanta as well as its birds, to give the illusion of windows. Philip Shutze thought of this unusual use of mirrored panels in the club and recommended Athos for the job.[8] An enormous undertaking for Sara, who assisted, the project should have taken six months to complete. Instead, the couple worked night and day to finish the 127 x 4 1/2-foot mural in two months on Thanksgiving Day 1939. Ironically, so intent were they in finishing the murals by this date that the only detail Athos omitted in his frenzied pace was his signature.

The premiere parties celebrating the movie version of Margaret Mitchell's best-selling novel *Gone With the Wind* were held in the very room Menaboni helped design. "Margaret Mitchell was a frequent visitor to the Capital City Club…since both her father and her brother were members. There was a special *Gone With the Wind* dinner dance on December 12, 1939, at 6:30 PM. And on Thursday and Friday December 14 and 15, 1939, the Club celebrated the much-heralded premiere with a cocktail party…and an 'Old Fashion' dinner-dance…in the 'new room' of the City Club."[9]

The Mirador Room's murals caused a sensation. The membership was so ecstatic about the beautiful reverse murals that Athos was given a life membership to the exclusive club after their completion. In an attempt to answer questions by curious onlookers as to the process by which Athos accomplished such beauty and perfection, Sara wrote:

> Probably Athos did not make sketches, for economy of time; I recall that he mentioned lots of native plants and birds, but kept secret his intention of surprising Shutze with the introducing of a non-native plant, a camellia bush in bloom, since Shutze loved and grew camellias. Also for economy of time, the Atlanta Glass Company sent the smallest glass panels to our studio, where Athos could paint them easier than having to go—as he did toward the last weeks—all the way into town to the Glass Company to work on the largest panels. Also, we had to work closely on a schedule with the Atlanta Glass Company, for after

the painting was done, with thinned oil pigments, and before the paint was covered with liquid nitrate of silver, every painted area had to be coated [using artist's paint brushes of all sizes] with varnish, and this varnishing was to be my job as [his] assistant. When the varnish was tacky to the touch of a finger, each panel would be laid on a perfectly flat table at the Glass Company and the nitrate of silver poured over it from a pitcher. If I had failed to varnish any stem or leaf or whatnot, the nitrate would remove the oil paint. Fortunately, we had good working relations with architects and workers, and not one thing went wrong, and we met all deadlines with cooperation from everyone.

Athos started the project by making the outlines of the plant and bird subjects on life-sized brown paper, but scarcely any details. I perforated the brown paper, in order for him to transfer the design…onto the glass. The finishing touches were painted on first, instead of the normal procedure of painting in a basic color and gradually adding shadow and light and working toward the way finished art would look to an audience. To see how he was getting along, the artist rigged up a large mirror on the other side to look into—but he found this to be hard on his eyes, for he was looking through the glass he was working on, to another glass surface, then back through his glass he was working on. He found it was more comfortable to occasionally walk around his glass to see what he had painted, and he discarded the mirror. I noted that he did not look often; Athos Menaboni simply knew what he was painting, whether backwards or forward or upside down![10]

More mural works followed as his reputation grew. He received commission offers throughout the United States. In Chatham, Virginia, he combined his love of all animals using predominant shades of green, orange, and blue to encircle the central figure of St. Francis of Assisi, who appears standing in the woods surrounded by small animals in the Lillian Hensleigh Memorial Mural in Chatham Hall. Reminiscent of old Italian mural work, this 1955 work portrays eighteen of the varieties of birds native to Virginia. All the trees and flowers in the mural are also native to Virginia.

The Capital City Club continued to support and patronize Menaboni, purchasing an additional six paintings in 1939. The artist himself was a volunteer in the Capital City Club development program in the early 1980s. Later, in the 1980s, this club also reproduced his artwork to adorn their dinner menu covers and emphasized their approval by displaying another of his works on the cover of the 1986 issue of the club magazine, *Seasons*, as well as writing stories highlighting his art in four issues of the magazine. In 1991, the mirrored panels were featured in the book *Capital City Club: The First One Hundred Years 1883-1983* by James C. Bryant.

Commercial Commissions with Citizens & Southern National Bank

A LONG-STANDING PERSONAL FRIENDSHIP AND working relationship with Mills B. Lane, Jr., president of Citizens and Southern (C & S) National Bank of Georgia began in the 1950s. In 1927, Athos's first year in Atlanta, he had opened his first bank account at this C & S bank. Working closely with Lane, who was responsible for hiring Athos on behalf of C & S Bank and other foundations with which he was affiliated, was another major force in catapulting his career.

In 1955, Lane commissioned Athos to design a set of dinner plates to solely benefit the Cerebral Palsy School-Clinic of Atlanta, of which he was a patron. The result was a white, limited-edition fine-china plate rimmed in gold. Each plate in the Menaboni "American Song Birds" series featured one of eight different song birds and a different flower.

The distinguished series was manufactured by Syracuse China in Syracuse, New York, and packaged in two sets of four that sold for twenty-five dollars per set. Set one of the dinner plates featured the Carolina Wren with Black-eyed Susan, the Eastern Bluebird with Pink Bindweed, Golden-crowned Kinglet with Blue Fringed

Gentian, and the Painted Bunting with Yellow Jasmine. Set two of the beautiful plates displayed the Cardinal with Brown Sweet Shrub, the Cedar Waxwing with Red Chokeberry, the Common Goldfinch (or wild canary) with Yellow Chicory, and the Indigo Bunting with Yellow Mellein. The twenty colors on the plates were so outstanding and complex in detail that Onodaga Pottery (part of Syracuse China) was unable to produce them and the Commercial Decal Company of Mt. Vernon, New York, was hired to produce decals for this exquisite series.

Because Syracuse China would accept only a minimum order of 6,000 dozen, 72,000 "American Song Bird" plates were manufactured. Plate sales would continue for the next ten years until the entire inventory was depleted. The head of Abercrombie and Fitch in New York was a friend of Mills B. Lane and helped his friend by letting his store handle the sale of some of the plates. The Cerebral Palsy School-Clinic of Atlanta made $190,000 from the sale of the song-bird plates. More than twenty years later, in 1978, after the series' success, Mr. Lane proposed a game bird plate series. This project never materialized.

In 1958 Athos produced a fabulous eggshell mosaic for the new Emory Branch of C & S Bank in Decatur, Georgia. His theme was the Biblical phrase, "Whatsoever a man soweth, that he shall also reap." Athos believed in and lived by this passage. This passage represented the core of the man. In three pictorial panels, the mural shows a man sowing his crop and the various stages of growth. Two panels of Japanese Nakora wood flanked the center unit in his design that features the four elements: fire represented by a torch, earth represented by a gazelle, air represented by birds, and water represented by fish.

The C & S Bank eggshell mural took ten months to complete. Done in 1 1/2 x 4 1/2-feet sections, its finished three panel design was 4 1/2 x 27 feet. The mural required over 266 dozen eggshells that were donated by a local restaurant. Sara peeled almost 3200 eggshell membranes and gave them to Athos to mount for this mural. Athos' sisters, Tina and Marguerita, were recruited to help peel the eggs. Athos fit eggshell fragments into place on top of an adhesive, with tweezers, piecing the shell fragments together on his design as one would place pieces in a jigsaw puzzle. He then used a rubber roller to secure the pieces in place. After all the eggshells were secure, Menaboni painted the mural design.

Inspiration for the eggshell mosaic, believed to be the only remaining one of its kind in the world, came from a book Athos purchased: *The Craftsman's Handbook*, the English translation of the Italian book, *Il Libro Dell'-Arte*, written in 1437 by Cennini Cennino D'Andrea. Many paragraphs were missing in the translated book, but enough remained to intrigue and inspire Athos. Not only did Athos complete the incredible mural in time for the bank's grand opening, he himself was present at the opening-day celebration to greet enthusiastic new patrons.

This triptych mural received much publicity and was featured in *This is Your Georgia* by Bernice McCullar, a school text book used in the state of Georgia. Menaboni stands in front of his completed mural in the text book. Many school-age children familiar with the artist's talent for healing birds became aware of his artistic talent through this book.

Branches of Citizens and Southern Bank across Georgia prominently displayed works by Menaboni in their lobbies and board rooms. In 1969, Athos painted a ten-foot-high, golden, mosaic mural that extended 110 feet around the central core of the North Avenue branch. On the top floor of the twenty-one story office tower (located on North Avenue at the intersection of West Peachtree Street in Atlanta) was the Commerce Club, a downtown businessman's luncheon club. Members and guests of the club were able to enjoy both a panoramic view of the city and Menaboni's mural depicting the local Georgia sourwood leaf. At the Mitchell Street branch, he painted a 648-square-foot-mural, the second largest in Atlanta at the time, inspired by a scene he had originally sketched in Cherokee County, Georgia. The young lad he painted in the foreground of the beautiful Georgia countryside mural was Mills B. Lane IV as a boy. Native birds, such as a Red-tailed Hawk, were pictured throughout the mural. For the Albany, Georgia, branch, Athos painted five murals and a painting he rendered of Wild Turkeys on Nakora wood hung in the lobby. In the Cherry Street branch in Macon, Georgia, Athos painted canvasses depicting significant events in Georgia history on the walls behind the tellers' line. At the Buckhead branch, he painted five panels of the rare Whooping Crane on horizontally grained African walnut, amidst cattails and sansevieria. The 5 x 6-foot panels depict the cranes in their true size.

In the late 1970s Athos was again commissioned by the North Avenue office and painted two botanicals: the Red Maple leaf and Tulip Tree leaf that hung in the lobby. Colored lithographs of the botanicals were later used in a special promotion and given to customers opening accounts at this C & S branch. The Red Maple leaf's significant contribution to graphic communication was noted and applauded, and Athos received a Graphic Arts Award for his outstanding design.

The Hatching of "The Birds"

IN THE DEPRESSION YEARS OF THE 1930s, WHEN mural commissions were scarce and considered a luxury that only a privileged few could afford, Athos spent time experimenting and painting for his own pleasure, combining the skills he had learned as a painter with his hobby, the study of birds. The work of John James Audubon motivated and roused him. A bird feeder Sara had placed outside his studio window fed a vast array of guests including Blue Jays, finches, and warblers, and these became his source of inspiration. He found birds intelligent, mysterious, gentle, and beautiful subjects.

It was during this free time that Athos painted his first serious bird painting, a pair of Cardinals for their living room wall. Sara never got a chance to hang it. While visiting the Menabonis at their home, decorator Molly Aeck said she had a client who would love the painting and took it immediately. This first bird study, purchased by Dr. and Mrs. Hartwell Boyd of St. Simons Island in 1938, was to be a major turning point in Athos's artistic career. He painted another bird portrait and then another and they each sold. His accurate portrayals of birds with artistic and decorative overtones in beautiful compositional designs made them highly desirable works of art.

Like Audubon, Menaboni painted his birds life-size with few exceptions. Also, he almost always painted birds as a pair. But unlike Audubon, who painted from recently-killed birds that he had wired into a pose, Menaboni worked predominantly from live-bird studies, thus he is referred to as a scientific ornithological painter. He painted a complete picture of wild bird life through his accurate and detailed painted physical descriptions. Only after years of experience did he paint from memory. Menaboni's birds are more than just accurate anatomical studies; his phenomenal knowledge of birds' bone structures and his impeccable sense of detail were exceptional. Observing a bird in the live state enabled him to capture its expressive eyes, natural appearance, exact coloration, prominent markings, plumage peculiarities, stance, personality, and attitude. He believed birds are like people—their faces are unique.

When news of Menaboni's bird paintings spread, his popularity grew and the commission work poured in faster than Athos could keep up with it. The names of patrons-to-be were added to a waiting list. At times, he was two years behind and Roger Tory Peterson, in his introductory remarks of the 1981 edition of *Audubon's Birds of America*, noted that Menaboni's clients would snatch up his works before the paint was dry. He was the South's premier bird painter and the most sought-after artist in Atlanta. He would sometimes work on three paintings at once, often remarking to friends that the day was never long enough. At one time, Athos produced forty paintings in four months. He could finish a simple gray bird in a day. Quail were most difficult for him to paint, requiring several days in order to capture their intricate feather pattern. Athos

Blue Jays and Snake, circa 1940

Wood Thrush, No. 76 A, circa 1940

Mourning Doves, circa 1950

Meadowlark, circa 1950

Bufflehead, circa 1950

Wood Duck, circa 1940

Brown Leghorn, circa 1950

Mallards, circa 1950

Evening Grosbeak with Blue-berried Dogwood, circa 1960

Snowy Egret, circa 1950

Magnolia, circa 1950

Mourning Dove, zenaidura macroura, circa 1950

Bobwhite, colinus virginianus, circa 1950

Florida Gallinule, circa 1950

Christmas Greenery, circa 1960

Mourning Doves on Nakora Wood,
circa 1960

Prunifolia Azalea, circa 1950

once said, "It took me three to four days to paint each original, but in another sense, it took a lifetime of learning how to paint."

He employed Italian glass, eggshells, watercolors, and pencil in his works, but painted almost exclusively in oils on a variety of mediums—glass, silk, wood panels, Masonite, mirrors, treated paper, and gesso-covered board. He also developed the aforementioned undercoat method. The undercoat method required Athos to cover his palette with several patches of paint and then allow them to dry. Then filling a brush with liquid solvent (usually kerosene), he dissolved a small amount of his dried color that he would then thin and apply to his primed paper. He did this repeatedly, creating layers of pigment with varying tones and colors. Another unique characteristic distinguishing his works is the fine line used to outline the central figure(s) of his paintings. This line, which is most often white, defines and separates his primary subjects from their immediate background.

In his tireless quest for perfection, Menaboni painted more than 150 species of American birds throughout his career, but never painted the same scene twice. "I love birds and I enjoy painting, so art is not work," Menaboni said. "It is a way of life."[11] He captured the beauty and drama of birds in flight, at rest, on branches, quarreling, nesting, and searching for food. Menaboni's cardinals and bluebird paintings were his best sellers; quail, dove, and duck paintings were also extremely popular commissions. Athos himself liked painting the Blue Jay and thought it quite a handsome species, but knew the public generally did not favor the jay because of its aggressive behavior. He had successfully raised a half-starved Blue Jay that a child once brought him, and fed it painstakingly and lovingly until it was healthy. "Jay, the Magnificent," the name Athos had given the orphan bird, continued to dine at the Menaboni window sill, long after he was "cured" on dishes Athos especially concocted for him long after he was cured. After this heartfelt experience, "Jay" and others of his kind held a special place in Athos's heart.

Finding certain birds he desired to paint was difficult. In the early 1930s, he wrote to the Smithsonian Institution seeking permission to collect one of each variety of birds that were protected by game laws. His intent was to use these birds as models for his pictures. By 1950, he had received permits to collect two of each species (a male and a female) a year for his work. Occasionally, he would trap birds, care for them, study their dimensions, colors and markings, and then set them free.

In order to accurately paint distinguishing marks—the precise feather arrangement and count that differentiated species—Athos would sometimes study a stuffed bird or carcass or appendages on loan from various museums—similar to borrowing from a lending library—such as the Cincinnati Museum of Natural Art. He did have a collection of bird mannequins around his studio and often kept skins in his refrigerator. One man recalled visiting Menaboni's studio as a mischievous little boy and opening a drawer he had been told was "off limits." In it, he was surprised to find an array of bird's feet, wings, beaks, and other anatomical parts which Menaboni used as models and references for his methodical work.

Neighbors brought Athos their pet birds to paint as well as nurse back to health. One such bird was a Red Macaw named Chou Chou, who had plucked out most of its feathers. The only feathers remaining were on its head with a few sparsely scattered on its tail. Athos could not paint Chou Chou in his sorry condition and thus went to the Atlanta Zoo to study Red Macaws. He did, however, study and paint the face of Chou Chou in order to capture his true character and personality and filled in his plumage in his painting as it should have appeared after his observations at the zoo. Chou Chou's plumage did improve under Athos's care and his owners were pleased to have a painting of the bird they remembered fully plumed. Another neighbor brought Athos a Ruby-throated Hummingbird that had died after flying into the neighbor's screened porch and getting its beak stuck. Athos did paint the hummingbird in several of his paintings and created a lovely and intimate lithograph to show this delicate species. Similarly, an injured Purple Gallinue he found near his property became his model and source of inspiration for his 1950 Woodruff Christmas card.

His bold and beautiful portrayals of his bird subjects in their natural habitat were rendered accurately and with perfect harmony. His excellent sense of balance can be attributed to his early training as a muralist. He was also meticulous to a fault. Though his clients chose the bird they wished to have painted, Athos always chose the flora to complement the subject—his knowledge of both was profound. Because of close observations, his paintings were faithful to his subjects, down to the last details. The foliage plays an important part in his compositions, but never overpowers the central figure. He did not portray nature as picture perfect, but reproduced it with uncompromising honesty, his paintings exhibiting a direct observation of nature. If the leaves he was using as models for his paintings were bruised or browning and chewed by caterpillars, that is what he painted.

In contrast, the famed John J. Audubon painted only the birds in his compositions, allowing apprentices to finish the background foliage that usually required as much time executing as the bird subjects required. Audubon's sons often helped with the foliage in his paintings and one of his sons even painted some of the birds in the

Audubon works. Athos had no apprentices or other assistants. Everything seen in his paintings, the beauty nature created, was carefully and tirelessly produced by the artist himself.

Friends often brought Athos living birds and flora so he could select subject and background material for his works. He frequently sent Sara on missions to find appropriate examples of the particular live flora he wished to paint. On one occasion, she went all over town searching for a specimen of magnolia leaves and buds, and she almost returned empty-handed, only to find the perfect specimen just two blocks from their home.

At times, he decided to change some of the backgrounds in his already completed paintings. He once changed an entire background in a raven painting, changing the seasons from summer to fall. He altered other works, such as one of his marine scenes in which he painted out the entire background so that only his boats remained. In one of his seacoast scenes, which hung in his dining room, he added a lighthouse years after its original completion.

Athos enjoyed creating personal projects, as well as those he was commissioned to paint. Visitors often wanted to buy paintings that were hanging on the walls of his home. For that reason alone, he had painted an enormous Turkey Vulture that hung over the mantle. The Turkey Vulture was not a desired commission and he often remarked that he painted the bird, not its odor. Eventually it, too, was purchased by a visitor to their home. He painted a single iris on silk that hung in Sara's bedroom and several marine scenes, with which he never parted, that hung in their dining and living room area. In his later years he enjoyed painting wooden decoy ducks. Most of these he did for friends or kept for himself.

Born and raised in front of the harbor, the sea was his first love. Reflecting this love of sailing and the sea were his many paintings offering views reminiscent of Italy and particularly his hometown of Livorno. Years after the artist's death, Tina Menaboni still lived with many of these Italian scenes in her living room that held dear memories for the homeland she had left decades earlier. He often took Sara and his sister Tina to watch the sailboats on Lake Lanier. When interviewed for a magazine story in his later years, Athos said the only thing he would have changed about his life was to have lived near the sea and have owned his own boat.

In the 1970s, scraps of Masonite that had leaned against his garage for nearly three years became another source of inspiration for his work. After withstanding the tests of time and the elements, the Masonite scraps seemed to Athos to be in perfect condition, and he decided it would be an excellent medium to work on because of its durability. He thought Masonite to be one of man's greatest inventions. He experimented, manipulating his oil pigments with palette knives and painting on both sides (the rough and the smooth) of his new-found medium. He believed that the Masonite's rough side mimicked the grain of canvas. On these paintings, he applied a heavier, more conventional amount of oil paint than he was generally accustomed to using. The end result of these rough side renderings lacked some of the fine feather detail for which he was known. The paintings done on the Masonite's smooth side were the most adaptable to his palette knife technique. These finished paintings captured magnificent details and resembled those executed on wood panels. Both the paintings executed on the smooth and rough sides, although vivid in themselves, do not have quite the luster and iridescence of his paintings on paper where he employed his perfected undercoat technique. These paintings were usually experimental and done for his own personal enjoyment, and they were never offered for sale.

Becolini, circa 1930

More of the Woodruff Connection

ALTHOUGH NOT FLYING ENTHUSIASTS, MR. AND Mrs. Robert Woodruff took an interest in the Coca-Cola corporate airplanes and commissioned Athos to paint many murals in the fleet. His work was usually overseen by Mrs. Woodruff. She generally chose what was to be painted, rather than have Athos paint her husband's subject choices. Before Athos began painting, the Coca-Cola Company supplied him with the fabric that was stretched and hung (similar to the method used in the Reynolds mansion murals on Sapelo Island) in the corporate airplane. The finished product always pleased Mr. Woodruff. The Coca-Cola Company had Menaboni paintings reproduced for their 1959 home calendar. The cover featured the Carolina Chickadee, while inside the calendar were six other beautiful reproductions of Menaboni's song birds. January/February's bird was the Cedar Waxwing, March/April's bird was the Bobwhite, May/June's was the Eastern Red-winged Blackbird, July/August's was the Eastern Bluebird, September/ October's featured the Grey-cheeked Thrush, and November/ December's picture was the Cardinal. "Play Refreshed" was another advertisement painted for the company reproduced in poster form in the 1950s and, in later years, post cards. This featured the famous Coca-Cola bulls-eye and Coca-Cola bottle surrounded by sports balls—a bowling ball, basketball, and others—along with Menaboni's unmistakable quail and ducks.

In the late 1970s, Robert Woodruff commissioned him to paint, this time on glass, a pair of Mallards in flight for the transom of the Woodruff Room in the Robert W. Woodruff Library at Emory University in Atlanta. Athos even designed the room's window drapery motif of reed grasses. Woodruff donated his original painting of *Snowy Egrets at Ichauway Plantation* that was lithographed for the family Christmas card in 1949 to the Woodruff Library's Woodruff Room.

The Woodruff's introduced their friends and fellow nature lovers Cason and Virginia Callaway to Athos's work in the 1940s. The Callaways had bought land in Pine Mountain, Georgia in 1930 for conservation and gardening endeavors. The property is now known as Callaway Gardens. The Callaways commissioned Athos to do many paintings for them and they formed a strong and lasting friendship with the artist. The Callaway children also became friends with Athos and Sara, who were frequent visitors to their parents' home. Cason's son and his spouse, Mr. and Mrs. Howard H. Callaway, vividly recalled that during one of Athos's visits, Mr. Carson Callaway promised the artist some Mallards which he could add to his flock at Valle Ombrosa. Upon Athos's return home, he waited patiently, and then anxiously, for their arrival. Some three weeks after his visit, the Mallards had still not arrived. Cason Callaway, who rarely forgot anything, let alone a promise, apparently did forget his promise to his good friend Athos. This prompted a good-humored joke on the part of Athos. Athos sent Virginia and Cason a Christmas card on which he had drawn a case of Mallards squawking. Mr. Cason Callaway responded immediately, sending Athos the desired Mallards. The families were very close and remained so. In their wills, Athos and Sara Menaboni left their entire estates, which included numerous paintings and sketches, to Callaway Gardens.

Blue Jays and Snake, circa 1940

Menaboni's Birds

IN THE 1940s, SARA AND ATHOS COMBINED
THEIR efforts while working for the *Atlanta Journal Magazine*.
Sara wrote many light-hearted articles about "birding" and life with
Athos, while Athos painted illustrations to accompany her stories
(as well as stories by others), which appeared in the *Atlanta Journal
Magazine* and on the magazine's cover. A picture taken of Athos's
painting that detailed two distressed Blue Jays who appear frantic as
a snake invades the privacy of their nest appeared on the cover of the
Atlanta Journal Magazine in 1945. Athos had observed this dramatic scene from his studio window before he captured it in paint. He
was able to seize the snake before any harm came to the jay's nest
and, after completing his painting, he and Sara took the snake to
Fernbank Science Center. This sense of immediacy and suspense in
the cover picture, caught the eye of John Selby, editor and chief with
Rinehart & Company, Inc. in New York, while on a visit to Atlanta.
Selby contacted Sara and Athos and encouraged them to collaborate
on a bird book, and they agreed.

Sara worked for three years recording their life, discoveries, travels, bird sightings, and bird stories—the result was *Menaboni's Birds*. Published in 1950 by Rinehart & Company, Inc. *Menaboni's Birds* was voted one of the fifty best books of the year by the American Graphic Society. It is a beautiful coffee-table book filled with illustrations done by Menaboni and thirty-two exquisite and brilliantly colored lithographs of his bird paintings. Sara and Athos were very proud of their work. The price of *Menaboni's Birds* was to be $10.00 but the 25,000 books ordered sold out before publication at a lower pre-publication price. Rich's and Davison's department stores, Miller's Bookstore in Buckhead, and several other book stores in downtown Atlanta hosted autograph receptions for their customers to meet the famed artist and his wife.

An additional 1,000 books were made into a deluxe, limited edition that included signatures by both Sara and Athos, as well as a separate folder containing thirty-one color plates featured in the book. The deluxe editions were numbered 1 through 500 and A1 through A500 and sold for $25.00. The first limited edition book was numbered A1 and inscribed, "To Molly and Dick [Aeck], who dreamed our house, then made it a reality! Your devoted Menabonis. Valle Ombrosa, November 10, 1950." It was signed by Sara Menaboni and Athos Menaboni. So exhausted were Sara and Athos after signing hundreds, if not thousands, of books, that they went to Havana, Cuba, for a long rest afterwards. Much to their surprise, they were recognized in Cuba and asked for signatures there as well.

In conjunction with the book, the thirty-two color prints that *Menaboni's Birds* featured were offered for sale as 2 x 2-inch slides for $10.50 by mail order. A European edition of *Menaboni's Birds* was published by London's Michael Joseph, Limited, for world-wide publication in 1952. The book's success financed an addition to the Menabonis' home—a glassed-in aviary complete with a pool and waterfall for the Menaboni's tame birds. They never parted with the famous Blue Jay painting that inspired the book, which was a personal favorite of Sara's and hung in the entry hall of their home.

Unfortunately, the original plates for *Menaboni's Birds* were lost at sea in an airplane crash near England and were never to be printed from again. *Menaboni's Birds* was rereleased in 1984 by Clarkson N. Potter, Inc., a subsidiary of Crown Publishers, with a new set of thirty-two full-color reproductions copied from original Menaboni paintings owned by private collectors. The second printing and those that followed kept the original text written by Sara. The color was not nearly as accurate or precise as the 1950 edition, and Sara and Athos were quite disappointed. Subsequently other publishers followed suit in the republication of *Menaboni's Birds*—some without consent from the authors. Nonetheless, the public was happy to have another chance to purchase and enjoy *Menaboni's Birds*. Clarkson N. Potter hosted a party at the Atlanta History Center on November 27, 1984, to celebrate the book's second printing, with a select group of Menaboni enthusiasts, admirers, and its members present. Friends remember Sara and Athos having a wonderful time at this event. Governor Joe Frank Harris declared November 27, 1984, as Menaboni Bird Day across Georgia.

Scarlet Tanager with Magnolia Leaves, circa 1960

Pedro

IN THE LATE 1960S, ATHOS AND SARA CONSPIRED on another book that they titled *Pedro*. Sara again wrote the text and Athos illustrated the tale, which told of the trials and tribulations of a Scarlet Tanager's migratory journey from South America to the United States. For five years Athos and Sara had enjoyed watching a Scarlet Tanager they called Pedro come and go at Valle Ombrosa. Athos and Sara had grown quite fond of the little bird that even joined them at meals. The sixth spring the tanager did not return. Athos and Sara were saddened but were inspired to collaborate on his story. They tried to imagine what pitfalls Pedro would come up against traveling such a great distance every spring and fall.

In the book, Pedro was the hero, almost a stunt flyer, overcoming the threats of villainous predators. A cat, a snake, an owl, and an eagle each tried their best to catch Pedro in this tale. Pedro even manages to stow away on a ship, hiding in the center of a life preserver, on his journey southward. Athos painted a series of fifty oil pictures and rendered many pencil sketches of the tanager's adventures as he flew home to Yucatan through Louisiana and other Southern states. At the time of its writing, the publishers felt it too sophisticated for children and too childish for adults and *Pedro* was not published.

Athos with Peacock painting, circa 1989

Blue Jay, No. 40A, circa 1940

Photograph of Athos painting *Night Heron with Spanish Moss,* circa 1960

Night Heron with Spanish Moss, circa 1960

Scarlet Tanager with Magnolia Leaves, circa 1960

Quail, circa 1960

Ruffed Grouse, circa 1960

Indigo Bunting, circa 1960

Cardinals in Magnolia, circa 1960

Cardinal with Maple Leaves, circa 1960

Northern Bobwhite, circa 1960

Mallards in Flight,
circa 1960

White-tailed Kite, circa 1960

Bluebirds, circa 1960

Mockingbird, Catbird and Brown Thrasher, No. 128, circa 1940

Whooping Crane, circa 1970

La Torre del Marzocco, dated 1979

Bicentennial Bald Eagle, dated 1976

Menaboni's Evolving Style

THERE IS NO WAY TO ACCURATELY CALCULATE THE number of works Athos Menaboni painted in his long lifetime or to positively date these works. It is probable that thousands of works were painted during his enormously prolific career. Sara and Athos kept detailed notes of every species of bird they ever spotted, but never concerned themselves with an accounting of each painting. Dates and numbers seemed of no consequence. Patrons, collectors, and friends often inquired as to the "history" of certain paintings. In response to one such inquiry, Sara Menaboni wrote on 2 February 1987:

Dear Betty,

Thank you! Both Athos and I appreciated your kind letter after you had viewed the Menaboni exhibition at the Swan Coach House Gallery recently.

You commented on some of your Menaboni original paintings being each numbered: "27A, 23C, 31C." At the beginning of his bird painting career—which we had no idea would last for the

rest of his life (he is now 91)—we had the idea that by numbering each one, we could keep up with who owned each picture,
but we gave up that idea after a few years of frantic record-keep-
ing. Therefore, your numbers indicate: "early Menabonis."

She added, "Maybe you will paste this letter onto the back of
one of your paintings, as someone (say, in 50 years!) will want to
know the same thing you asked now!" [12]

Examining the paper used by Menaboni and his signature style
offers a means of dating his works. The details of the birds' feet in
his paintings are also key in determining a date for his works. In the
1940s, 1950s, and early 1960s, the feet he painted are incredibly
detailed and the viewer can almost feel the tough cartilage, joints,
and the sharpness of the razor-edged talons of his subjects. Into the
1970s, his birds' feet are lacking the superb detail of earlier years.
Into the 1980s and 1990s, the birds' feet are often not visible at all.
Instead, they are carefully and inconspicuously hidden behind the
foliage in his works. His depth perception was affected drastically by
a cataract in one of his eyes in his later years. As his eyesight became
worse, it was necessary for him to devote four months to perfecting
a painting that would, in earlier years, have required less than a
week's work. A brilliant Peacock painting done for Richard Kessler,
founder of Enterprise Bank, was done during this period. Athos
painted it slowly and masterfully with one eye closed at the age of
ninety.

Initially, in the late 1920s, Athos painted on wartime paper or
illustration board. He printed his signature in oil and under this
script added the year his painting was completed. Most often his
early paintings were landscapes and seascapes. His earliest ornithological works featured a single bird rather stiffly posed amidst a

simplistic floral background. The background in many of these early paintings has become somewhat discolored over time due to oxidation from sunlight. He started numbering his works in the early 1930s and 1940s and framed the works in with a fine pencil line. Under his subject he printed the bird's ornithological name and common name in pencil and then signed his name in pencil.

After a few years of experimenting, by the early 1940s, Athos grew more comfortable in his art. He began painting birds as a pair, and the stiffness in his works is considerably less, giving way to a more fluid, three-dimensional, and animated representation of his subjects. About this time, he stopped numbering his paintings, finding it too cumbersome a task. Although he also discontinued framing his paintings with the pencil line, he continued for some time to put the name of the bird in pencil at the bottom of his works.

At some point, probably in the late 1940s to early 1950s, Menaboni started signing his name in paint. His linear pencil signature took on a slightly different appearance, becoming bolder and more rounded, yet retaining his unmistakable script. He was so adept at signing his name with a paintbrush that he once had to sign a check in paint, because he could not find a pen. Some of the brushes he used for extra fine details had only one or two bristles. So unique was Menaboni's signature that it became part of an exhibit of distinct signatures at Emory University in the early 1970s. Among other signatures in the exhibit were those of President Harry S Truman, poet Robert Frost, President Abraham Lincoln, Samuel Clemens (Mark Twain), Joel Chandler Harris, Theodore Roosevelt, and Winston Churchill.

After 1950, Athos began priming his illustration paper with gesso to protect against aging. Soon he started painting on Morilla Bond

Athos's signature has a distinct style

watercolor paper, and later he applied three thin layers of gesso to the paper as a primer. This priming gave the proper background for some of his most impeccably detailed and vivid works.

Collectors and ornithologists, wildlife lovers, and naturalists alike generally agree that Menaboni painted his finest and most meticulously detailed works in the 1940s, 1950s, and the early 1960s—the peak of his illustrious career. It was during this era that Menaboni was gaining worldwide fame. His clients included President Dwight D. Eisenhower, the DuPonts, Marshall Fields, and other notables. His commissions came from as far away as Belgium, Italy, Scotland, Japan, and South Africa. Praised for his accurate representations, *Time* wrote a feature about the artistic genius of Athos Menaboni in 1950, stating that he was a better bird painter than Audubon because his details were more accurate. Others concurred and wrote that Menaboni was a better draftsman and colorist than Audubon. *Time* also noted that Menaboni's paintings captured the metallic sheen of the birds' plumage while Audubon's did not. The wonderful sheen, iridescence, and exquisite texture of his birds' feathers rendered with extreme precision was a distinct quality that separated him from other capable bird painters of his time. Through his delicate brush strokes, his paintings convey the texture and lightness of bird feathers. His brilliant use of realistic and radiant colors, and the shadows and highlights he expertly contrasts, heighten the effect of light in his renderings. Roger Tory Peterson, celebrated painter and author of the acclaimed *Field Guide to Birds*, pointed out that one of Menaboni's special features was his exceptional feather technique, which put him in a class by himself.

Recognizing how much his art had progressed, Athos told friends that he wished he could gather up all his early works and burn them because the bird subjects seemed so rigid and the execution was so inferior to what he had become capable of painting. Years after reaching the height of his fame, he said, "The old masters continued to develop as long as they lived. The life of a man is short. When you start really knowing something, it's time to go."[13]

During a three-month visit to Japan with Sara in 1959, he attended art classes in Tokyo. He studied the fine brush technique and spacing and compositional refinements of Japanese art. His lessons had a profound and lasting impact on his work. His style, in turn, reflected the simplistic influences, graceful techniques, and elegance of old Japanese art. As a result of his trip to Japan, and his constant quest for new innovative techniques, he "discovered" and became fascinated with Nakora wood as a medium for his work. He found this wood to be ideal to paint on because its unique wood grain resembled features such as rippling water, which he could incorporate into his paintings in a multitude of ways. No two pieces of the Japanese plywood (which is no longer available) were alike. He became a technical master with the wood and said, "I keep seeing pictures in this wood."[14] On this medium, he painted birds swimming amidst the Nakora's rippling grain and resting atop the water's surface represented by the grain. Often, the wood grain was incorporated into his bird's plumage as well. Many of his paintings from the 1960s and into the 1970s were painted on this wood. Two of the

Christmas cards Athos painted for Robert Woodruff were also painted on this wood: the 1962 card featuring a Mallard at Ichauway Plantation and the 1963 card rendition of a Summer Tanager in dogwood at Ichauway Plantation. In addition to learning the art of painting on wood, the trip to Japan offered Athos the chance to learn the art of painting on Shiki silk. It was after this trip that he painted seven large sliding screen panels markedly similar to Japanese screens for Lockheed Aeronautical Systems, Inc., in Marietta, Georgia. His profound Oriental influence is marked in the decorative qualities of each panel measuring 108 x 51 inches. His work, *A Tree in Autumn with Birds,* beautifully depicts birds against a leafy backdrop, and is especially significant because the moveable screen provides a means of preservation for his work. Several years later, in a letter expressing birthday wishes to the artist, Lockheed Aeronautical Systems president W. P. French wrote, "We at Lockheed have conceived even bigger and stronger aluminum winged birds over the years. Our techniques have progressed from drafting boards to computers. But I doubt that we ever will achieve the grace and beauty of your creations."

Menaboni's Agents

REALIZING THE NEED TO PROMOTE ATHOS'S WORK outside Atlanta, the Menabonis worked out an arrangement with Lester Kierstead Henderson in the late 1960s. Henderson, a wealthy collector and owner of the Henderson Galley of Fine American Art in Monterey, California, traveled the country in his private jet promoting and exhibiting his clients' works as well as taking family portraits. When Athos found spare time between commissions he busied himself painting bird portraits of his choice. Once completed, these were then shipped to Henderson to add to his collection. Henderson frequently exhibited Menaboni's work, and generally sold each bird painting for $5,000 to $6,000. Athos received approximately $2,500 from each sale. Henderson remained Menaboni's agent until Henderson's failing health in the late 1980s forced him to liquidate many of his assets, including his Menaboni collection of approximately forty bird paintings. Most of these paintings made their way back to Atlanta through Henderson's dealing with Dave Knoke, an avid collector and owner of Knoke Galleries of Atlanta.

While Henderson handled Menaboni sales on the West Coast, the Menabonis retained the sole right to sell paintings east of the Mississippi with the exception of their agent in New York. Little is known about Menaboni's New York agent who, like Henderson, also charged $5,000 to $6,000 for each painting. Athos again received approximately half of each sale price as his fee for each work sold.

Sara would have preferred not to involve any agent with the sale of her husband's work. She hoped to be the one to bring her beloved husband the worldwide attention he deserved. In handling the majority of Menaboni painting sales, Sara generally set a standard fee for Athos's commissions, never pricing them very high, regardless of their specific subject matter. She was proud of a client having what she referred to as a "Menaboni Original," and she appreciated each client's interest in her husband's work. She had a very lenient and flexible payment plan for the bird portraits, allowing a client as long as needed to make payment in full. In the meantime, the client was able to take his painting home to enjoy while paying off the balance due.

While "eking" out a living, or as Sara believed "making a name for himself," Athos often made unannounced house calls. Collectors recall the "bird man" knocking at their door in the early 1940s with a completed painting in hand for immediate sale. At the time, his asking price was only $100 to $200. Only a short while later, he was earning $400 to $500 for his commissioned paintings, a considerable sum in his early years. The last price charged was about $2,000 in the early 1980s though paintings brought as much as $5,000 or more on occasion.

Other Private and Commercial Print Work and Commissions

THROUGHOUT MUCH OF THE 1940s AND 1950s, Athos also worked for many large corporations. Athos's talent knew no limits and he often remarked, "If it is done with paint and brushes, I do it." Independently, under Sara's guidance, Athos also had prints produced of several of his paintings. Framed Menaboni prints grace homes throughout the world.

The Southern Spring Bed Company of Atlanta was among the first to use Menaboni's artwork (lithographs of the *Blue Jay* and the *Red-headed Woodpecker*) in 1942 as a promotional feature in their sales campaign. "The Brighter the Home, the Better the Morale" was their slogan that stated,

> War is grim business, but Victory cannot be won in an atmosphere of gloom. Heads up—chins up—that's the formula we follow in our homes to fire us with zeal for our civilian duties to inspire our loved ones on our country's far-flung battle fronts. Accept with our compliments this contribution to that purpose—two prints of inspiring color for your home. Faithfully

executed by the gifted brush of Athos Menaboni who has been lauded by a host of art critics as America's foremost painter of birds, these exquisite prints are now available by exclusive arrangement only to purchasers of Southern Cross bedding product. We hope you will like the prints and that they will serve as a constant reminder of the beauty and softness of Southern Cross bedding products....

Menaboni's works appeared in a number of other commercial and noncommercial projects as well. The National Audubon Society endorsed four Menaboni prints produced for Quaker State Lithographing Company, Inc., in 1943. These subjects were the Green-winged Teal, the Bufflehead, the Bobwhite, and the Valley Quail. Two more prints, *The Hooded Merganser* and *The Wood Duck*, were done in 1945. In the mid 1940s, Menaboni executed four prints for Friendly Shoes, a subsidiary of Edgewood Shoes in Atlanta. The subjects were a Cardinal, an Evening Grosbeak, a Blue Grosbeak, and a Rose-breasted Grosbeak. A set of these prints was available for twenty-five cents with the purchase of every pair of Friendly Shoes. The only bird pictured in *Birds of Georgia: A Preliminary Check-List and Bibliography of Georgia Ornithology*, published in 1945 by the University of Georgia Press, was a Great Blue Heron reproduced monochromatically from a painting by Athos.

Menaboni contracted with Foote & Davies, Inc., of Atlanta in the early 1940s to make prints of the beautiful Chinese Hibiscus he had painted. Lithographed in 1945, the hibiscus was to be the first in a series of flower prints, but no others were ever produced. The sales and distribution of these prints, as well as other prints, such as *The Red-winged Blackbird* and *The Cardinal* in 1948 which he had his sisters color by hand to give them something to do shortly after their arrival from Cuba, were all published by Foote & Davies. Sales were handled by Sara, and prints were available at Davison's department store. For a twelve dollar fee, a customer was able to purchase a hand-colored print measuring 20 x 26 inches, which had been auto-graphed by the artist himself. Again, in the late 1940s, Foote & Davies also produced another beautiful pair of lithographs for Athos. The subjects were the Red-headed Woodpecker and the Blue Jay. These were the same subjects used in the 1942 promotion by Southern Spring Bed Company but they were produced on a dif-ferent grade of paper.

His 1950 advertisement for the Prudential Life Insurance Company was voted one of the fifty best advertisements of the year by the American Society of Graphic Arts, and gave his commercial work a tremendous boost. For the ad, which was also produced as a small print, he painted a robin hovering over her nest feeding her fledglings. Under his painting, the caption read, "What will happen to your family when you are gone?" The painting was criticized originally because the people at Prudential did not think the robin's red breast was red enough. Athos assured his critics that indeed the coloring was correct and, to prove further his point, pulled a robin mannequin out of his coat pocket. The red in the painting was indeed perfect. Additionally, he received the Award of Merit from the New York Art Directors Club for this painting.

After this celebrated ad many other companies, especially those in the Atlanta area, sought him out. Athos was given a commission from a candy company to paint a picture of a chocolate bar filled with peanuts. A friend of his was originally hired for the project, but was so consumed with other work that he had recommended Athos for the job instead. When Athos showed his painting of the company's candy bar, loaded with peanuts, to the company executives they told him they disliked it and asked him to redo the piece by adding more peanuts. Feeling completely dejected, Athos left the office and called the same friend who had recommended him for the job for advice. His friend told him that these executives acted like that all the time. His advice to Athos was to leave his painting alone, not alter it in the least, wait three or four days, and then take the original painting back to show them. Athos followed his friend's advice. The company executives took one look at the painting three days later and told Athos that was more like it—they loved it.

Montag Stationery contracted Athos to portray eight bird paintings from which they produced prints later in the 1950s. As a special promotional bonus each customer purchasing a box of the new line of featured stationery, received a Menaboni bird print, which was attached to the new stationery's box top. The subjects in these prints were the Carolina Chickadee, the Hooded Warbler, the Rose-breasted Grosbeak, two renditions of the Ruby-throated Hummingbird and the Ruby-crowned Kinglet, the Painted Bunting, and the Cardinal. Paintings of the Redstart and the Indigo Bunting were also executed by Athos and lithographed at about the same time and used to decorate stationery box tops.

The complete series of five menu covers he rendered for the Magnolia Room, the restaurant of the downtown Rich's department store, were displayed in the Georgia Exhibit at the Library of Congress in Washington, DC. Two of the covers, one depicting a deer and the other depicting seagulls, were black and white pencil sketches which first appeared in *Never the Nightingale*, a book published in 1951, written by Georgia poet laureate Daniel Whitehead Hicky, and illustrated by Athos. That same year he illustrated *Word*

This deer illustration was one of five menu covers used by the Magnolia Room at Rich's department store. It also appeared in *Never the Nightingale*, published in 1951.

Bouquets, a book of poetry written by Sallie Bass Arnold, a direct relative of his wife Sara. The other three menu covers are colored lithographs of Menaboni's paintings of the Cardinals, the Brown Thrasher, and the Cotton Blossoms, and all were printed by the Champion Paper & Fibre Company in Hamilton, Ohio. Rich's also had an exhibit of twenty-two of his bird originals in the Magnolia Room. Another major store, Davison's, commissioned Athos to paint their tearoom, the Terrace Restaurant, in 1951. He did, painting brightly-colored toucans and other South American birds.

The World Book commissioned Athos to illustrate their encyclopedia entry of American birds in 1957. Again in 1962, Athos collaborated on another bird entry with Arthur Singer, painting fifteen birds of the world. In "Hunters of the Sky," the Osprey and the Peregrine Falcon were illustrated, among others. The "Game Bird" pages showed illustrations of the Wild Turkey and the Prairie Chicken, while the "Water Birds" featured illustrations of the California Gull and the Great Blue Heron. The "Wild Duck and Wild Geese" pages featured illustrations of the Mallard and the Canvasback.

Employers Reinsurance Company of Atlanta also commissioned Athos to create six bird paintings. For this job he rendered paintings of game birds and birds of prey—Mallards, Canada Geese, Bald Eagle, Pheasant, Ducks, Red-tailed Hawk—that were reproduced as small prints for promotional use. Athos also did work for the Georgia Department of Natural Resources on small prints with a company advertisement generally located at the bottom of his featured art work.

Mary Mobley, owner of a frame shop by the same name, owned four Menaboni paintings that she had reproduced as full-color lith-

This illustration of seagulls was one of five menu covers used by the Magnolia Room at Rich's department store. It also appeared in *Never the Nightingale*, published in 1951.

ographs by the Preston Rose Company of Atlanta. In 1956, both *The Brown Leghorn* and *The Black Minora* were produced and in 1962 *The Bobwhite* and *The Mourning Dove* were lithographed. All four prints were available for sale to the public in two sizes.

An unnamed client commissioned Athos to paint a pair of life-size American Bald Eagles for the total fee of $2,000 in 1963. The 4 x 6-foot painting executed on Japanese Nakora plywood shows two eagles, one in flight and one perched on a limb. The unnamed client(s) turned out to be several of his close friends, including Richard Aeck, the architect who had designed his home. They had taken it upon themselves to secretly contact the mayor in Athos's hometown of Livorno and arrange to donate a Menaboni painting to their museum. Athos was kept in the dark about the arrangement because his friends feared that if he had known the painting was for his hometown, he would have insisted upon donating it. The unknown client was such a well-guarded secret, that when Athos found out who had participated in the commission, which his friends referred to as the "Menaboni Project", he called it "the best kept secret since the atomic bomb." The painting was donated and hung in a public gallery in Livorno.

The Memory Book, a last gathering of occasional verse written by Emory University English professor Thomas B. English in 1983, features on its cover a pine cone and spray of pine drawn by Athos. In the mid 1960s, Athos had painted two panels on Nakora wood for Wesley Woods, the north Georgia Conference retirement facility in Atlanta, where his friend Thomas English lived. On one panel, he rendered California Gulls and on the other the Little Blue Heron. These two panels that flanked a ten-foot-tall bird cage suspended from the ceiling were the largest known bird murals painted on wood. It was Thomas English who had edited *Menaboni's Birds* for Sara.

General James C. Grizzard, Athos's longtime friend and neighbor, helped bring Athos's work to many public exhibits in Georgia, most notably Jekyll Island. Through his service with the Jekyll Island Arts Association, Grizzard arranged an exhibit of Menaboni's paintings in 1974. General Grizzard orchestrated production of 250 *Snowy Egrets*, a limited edition, 20 x 24-inch lithograph, printed by Conyer Company Printing of Atlanta. The original piece was owned by General Grizzard and featured in the exhibition. They

Athos with Sara, 1987

were offered to the public for twenty-five dollars. Proceeds from the sale of these prints went to benefit the Jekyll Island Arts Association for educational and cultural projects. Years later, Athos presented a painting of an Osprey to the association in memory of a well-known ornithologist, and lifetime member of the association.

In 1975 General Grizzard commissioned Athos to paint an American Bald Eagle for the American bicentennial. The 24 x 36-inch painting was executed on Masonite and signed and dated by the artist. A limited number of signed and numbered 22 1/2 x 30-inch prints of the *Bicentennial Bald Eagle* were offered to the public in 1976 for a fee of $100. Most of the 950 prints were turned over to the Georgia Department of Education and distributed to public schools.

Ben Sims, a substantial member of the Atlanta community in the gardening realm, commissioned Athos to render twenty paintings of birds native to the state of Georgia in 1978. He, in turn, donated these paintings to the Atlanta Historical Society, in memory of his first wife, Margaret Demmon Sims. The bird subjects painted were the Bobwhite with Mullein, the Brown Thrasher with Cherokee Rose, the Red-winged Blackbird with Arrowhead, the Towhee with Thistle, the Barred Owl with Climbing Hydrangea, the Snowy Egret with Marsh Grass, the American Kestrel with White Pine, the Killdeer with Sand Dunes and Marsh Grass, the Wood Duck with Cypress and Spanish Moss, the Least Tern, the Eastern Bluebird with Red Maple, the Cardinal with Magnolia Grandiflora, the Black-capped Chickadee with Rock Chestnut Oak, the Blue Jay with Mountain Laurel, the Hooded Merganser with Marsh Grass, the Purple Gallinule with Marsh Grass, the Pileated Woodpecker with Dead Branch, the Wood Thrush with Maple-leaf Viburnum, and the Boat-tailed Grackle with Cat-tail. Ben Simms, along with over 700 other admirers of the Menabonis, attended the reception at the Atlanta History Center's McElreath Hall to celebrate the opening of the twenty-painting exhibit on December 3, 1979. In 1986 lithographs were made from two paintings, *The American Kestrel with White Pine* and *The Wood Duck with Spanish Moss*, and sold exclusively by the Atlanta History Center for seventy-five dollars. Originally they were signed and numbered by Athos but this practice was short-lived. In order to have the artist autograph the works, a history center representative would bring purchased prints to the Menaboni home for Athos to sign and number them. Sara, always the business woman, charged three dollars for each signature.

After much coercion by friends to try his hand at designing the Federal duck stamp in 1979, Athos painted two 5 x 7-inch paintings, *The Bufflehead Duck* and *The Ring-necked Duck*, for possible entry in the Federal Duck Stamp contest sponsored by the United States Postal Service. He chose to submit one, *The Bufflehead Duck*, for consideration. Another artist had previously submitted the same duck a year earlier, unbeknownst to Athos, so Athos's painting was not considered for selection.

In the late 1980s, Richard Kessler, founder of Enterprise Bank of Georgia, commissioned Athos to paint a large canvas of a sailing ship as an emblem for the first of his banks. The fictitious ship he painted was called the *Enterprise* and became the symbol of the bank. Lithographs were made of this painting and offered as gifts to the first 1,000 persons who opened accounts in 1987-1988.

This Mockingbird illustration was one of a limited edition of numbered lithographs printed in 1973. It was also used on the Atlanta Music Club program covers the same year.

Paintings, Murals and Prints for Charity

DESPITE THEIR BUSY CAREERS, ATHOS AND SARA kept active in their Atlanta community as well as serving as chairmen of various groups. One of these groups was the Georgia Committee of the Florentine Relief Fund, Inc., for which Sara served as chairman in 1967. The efforts of this group raised money to restore treasured art that had been damaged by flooding in Florence, Italy. Athos was extremely generous of his time and talents, making many contributions to noble causes, donating many signed prints and paintings to organizations in which he believed. He also donated many paintings in memory of dear friends.

Athos illustrated three catalogs printed for the American Camellia Society in 1949, 1950, and 1951, each titled *The American Camellia Catalog.* Only 1000 copies of these rare treasures were published in each of the three years, which each included numerous intimate studies of the flora by Menaboni. Camellia specimens were flown to him from Mississippi, Florida, and Georgia for use as his models. His paintings were made into lithographs and then hand-colored by students at the University of Georgia. He later sold these paintings privately. In the mid 1950s, the Kennedy Galleries, Inc., of New York offered fifty of Menaboni's original Camellia paintings for sale, with prices starting at $125. By the 1990s, the value of these high-ly desired paintings appreciated well into the thousands of dollars.

In 1959, Menaboni donated to the Cerebral Palsy School of Atlanta a 45,000-piece glass mosaic, *Earth and Sky*, in memory of his mother. The finished piece, thought to be the largest mural made with glass in existence, was 14 x 6 1/2 feet and covered seven panels. Requiring two and a half months of labor to complete, it shows fish in water, and birds on land and in the air. The glass for this spectacular mural came from Murano, Italy.

In 1970, Athos donated a painting to the Thomasville Arts Guild in memory of John Hashagen, the ship captain with whom he trav-eled to the United States in 1920. The captain and his wife retired to Thomasville, Georgia. Their close proximity making it easy for Athos to keep in touch with them. Athos donated other paintings in memory of special friends. He also donated a painting to Sara's alma mater, Shorter College in Rome, Georgia, as a tribute to her.

At the age of seventy-eight, Athos painted a monochromatic oil of a singing Mockingbird. A limited edition of 150 signed and num-bered lithographs (15 x 20 inches) was produced in 1973. The fifty dollar purchase price benefited the Atlanta Music Club and the *Mockingbird* was used for their program covers the same year. Earlier in the mid 1960s, he had designed the cover for their yearbook, and also as designed a cover for the 1965 yearbook.

In 1989, Athos donated a signed *Bicentennial Bald Eagle* print to benefit Georgia's Nongame Wildlife Conservation Fund. The print was auctioned at a fund-raiser at the Cloister. Key speaker for the event was naturalist, explorer, and host of television's *Mutual of Omaha's Wild Kingdom*, Jim Fowler.

Magazines

ATHOS EXPERIENCED MUCH SUCCESS AS AN illustrator. The many magazines for whom he illustrated covers in the 1940s and 1950s frequently ran stories about him and presented his work to a wide audience throughout the country. His prolific magazine work showed his accurate portrayals of song birds, game birds, birds of prey, and botanicals. His work also appeared on the covers of many arts center publications in the South. Magazines featuring his work were *Florida Wildlife*, *Progressive Farmer*, *Audubon*, *Outdoor Georgia*, *Sports Afield*, *Arizona Highways*, and *Georgia Game & Fish*, *Sports Illustrated*, *Georgia Life*, *Southern Accents*, and *Decor*.

A Mallard painted by Athos was featured on the November 15, 1954, cover of *Sports Illustrated*. Included in this issue was a series of sixteen pictures of ducks painted by Athos. Among the portraits featured were those of the Redhead, the Pintail, and Green-winged Teal. Athos not only rendered the Chukar Partridge appearing on the cover of the October 10, 1955, issue, but also six pages of game birds featured inside this issue as well. Harry Phillips, publisher of *Sports Illustrated*, wrote, "Athos Menaboni stands today among the top living portrayers of bird life as firmly as John James Audubon, who died over 100 years ago, stands for the best and finest in the long tradition of bird painting."[15]

Southern Accents magazine featured an article about Menaboni and showed several of his paintings including the *Evening Grosbeak* with *Blue-berried Dogwood* and *Cedar Waxwings* in the 1989 November/December issue.

The July 1956 *Progressive Farmer* cover featured a delightful Menaboni rendering of hummingbirds and morning glories set against a pale yellow background. Colored lithograph prints of this painting were offered by *Progressive Farmer*. One dollar was charged for one 22 x 26-inch print or three prints could be purchased for two dollars. Lithographs of pink, red, and white Chinese Hibiscus were also offered for sale at another time in addition to prints of Menaboni's flowers: crepe myrtle, azaleas, camellia, and lilac, as well as prints detailing dogwoods, pink azaleas, and forsythia.

The May 1968 *Decor* magazine featured four lithographs done from Menaboni's paintings: *The Brown Leghorn*, *The Black Minora*, *The Bobwhite*, and *The Mourning Dove*. Original prices for a 20 x 26-inch lithographs was $7.50, and a 12 x 18-inch print was offered for $3.75.

Menaboni's *Purple Martins* graced the cover of the winter 1976 issue of *Georgia Life*. This print was first used by Robert W. Woodruff for his Christmas card in 1951. Inside this issue was an article written by Charles Elliot about the birds at Ichauway Plantation. It included several reproductions from the Woodruff card series.

Conclusion

GIFTED ARTIST ATHOS MENABONI DIED JULY 18, 1990, at the age of ninety-four due to complications from a stroke suffered on May 25, 1990. His body was donated to Emory University. A memorial service was held July 22, 1990, at the Ida Cason Callaway Memorial Chapel at Callaway Gardens in Pine Mountain, Georgia. The chapel, in the midst of an exquisite garden, was a wonderful and fitting setting for the service of the man who loved nature so much. Printed on the memorial service program was the passage from Galatians 6:7 that Athos lived by—"Whatsoever a man soweth, that he shall also reap"—the same passage he had executed in his eggshell mosaic for Citizens and Southern Bank thirty-two years earlier. The First Lady of Georgia, Elizabeth Harris, delivered the eulogy at the service. Sara followed her beloved Athos in death three years later on August 10, 1993.

Works by Athos Menaboni appear in major museums and in some of the finest private collections in the United States and throughout the world. Menaboni collectors included former President Dwight D. Eisenhower, Robert W. Woodruff, Marshall

Field, the DuPonts, and the Callaways. Athos Menaboni painted for individuals and corporations, as well as sculpting and painting personal projects. This remarkable man began painting at the age of nine and continued until his death. He completed his last painting two weeks before his death. An unfinished portrait of sea gulls rested on his easel the day he died.

He believed art required training, skill, practice, and experimentation. He was always seeking new techniques and approaches to his art. He was a student of his craft as well as a master of it. His aesthetically-pleasing and life-like paintings appeal to wildlife lovers, naturalists, art collectors, and ornithologists alike. Many artists have been inspired by the artistic genius of Menaboni and his characteristic style. After all of his monumental accomplishments, the world should know Athos Menaboni.

In his obsession for perfection, Athos Menaboni captured the intimate spirit of his subject with a passion unequaled by other wildlife artists of his time. Menaboni shares with his viewer his fervent love for those things that meant everything to him—wildlife and nature. His life goes on in his works. His paintings are his treasures—his legacy. We, the viewers, are his heirs.

Exhibits and Awards

ATHOS MENABONI'S WORKS HAVE BEEN EXHIBITED at large art and natural history museums around the world, and in many smaller museums throughout the Southeast such as the Columbia Museum of Art, Pensacola Art Center, Callaway Gardens, the Swan Coach House (Atlanta), Marietta/Cobb Museum of Art, Albany Museum of Art, and the Emory University Woodruff Library. Major exhibits were held at the National Audubon Society, the Kennedy Art Galley, the Vose Galley, the St. Louis Art Museum, Atlanta's High Museum of Art, the American Museum of Natural History, the Seattle Art Museum, the Santa Barbara Museum, the Detroit Art Museum, and the Cincinnati Art Museum.

In his celebrated career, Menaboni received prestigious honors from the American Graphic Society, the Georgia Writers Association, the New York Art Directors Club, the American Institute of Graphic Arts, the Atlanta Beautiful Commission, the Capital City Club of Atlanta, and the American Institute of Architects; he also received the Georgia Governor's Award in Visual

Arts. Other awards bestowed upon him from organizations in metropolitan Atlanta were the Americanism Medal presented by the Joseph Habersham Chapter of the Daughters of the American Revolution, the Italian Cultural Society Committee Award, and the Award of Merit Certificate, the highest honor given by the Garden Club of Georgia, Incorporated.

Appendix

Menaboni art appearing on the cover and/or inside the *Atlanta Journal Magazine* and *Atlanta Journal & Constitution Magazine* (*AJC Magazine*) include:

Issue/Date:	Subject/Article Title:
February 25, 1945	Blue Jays and snake
April 15, 1945	Golden-crowned Kinglets and dogwood
November 24, 1946	Turkey
January 12, 1947	Blue Jay in dogwood
May 15, 1949	Brown Thrasher and Cherokee Rose
August 7, 1949	Scarlet Tanager in Magnolia
November 5, 1950	Battling Blue Jays
January 13, 1952	"Many Waters"
April 19, 1953	Etowah Indians
December 12, 1954	Brown Leghorn
September 16, 1956	Mockingbird in holly
November 15, 1959	Cerebral Palsy School-Clinic's glass mosaic
May 29, 1963	American Eagles
December 12, 1984	Raven

Articles written by Sara Menaboni for the *Atlanta Journal Magazine* that include illustrations by Athos Menaboni:

February 11, 1940	"Birds are Such Fun"
August 25, 1940	"Ducks Hatched on a Hot Pad"
January 12, 1941	"Owls are not Evil"
April 5, 1942	"Escape to Nature"
February 25, 1945	"How Menaboni painted the Battling Blue Jays"
January 27, 1946	"In Defense of Hawks and Owls"
September 15, 1946	"White Bluebirds and Red-tailed Hawks"
January 12, 1947	"A Bird in the Brush"
June 22, 1947	"It's Easy to Own Birds"
April 4, 1948	"Menaboni's Chicken Paintings"
July 18, 1948	"Vacationing with a Baby Robin"
July 10, 1949	"Playing Possum at the Menaboni's"
June 11, 1950	"How the Menaboni's Tamed a Hawk"

Magazine illustration work appears in the following:

Magazine:	Date, Subject/article title:
Arizona Highways	December 1973
Audubon Magazine	May/June 1956, Flickers July 8, 1973, "Valley of the Birds"
Decor	May 1968 of *The Brown Leghorn*, *The Black Minora*, *The Bobwhite*, and *The Mourning Dove*
Georgia Game & Fish	Fall 1950, Red-winged Blackbird and Snowy Egrets
Georgia Life	Winter 1976, Purple Martins
Georgia Magazine	December 1958/January 1959, "Eggshell Mosaic Something New in Art"
Nature Magazine	March 1942, "Living with a Marmoset"
Outdoor Georgia	October 1940, Hooded Merganser
Progressive Farmer	April 1947, favorite southern birds
	March 1948, Quail, Robins and Mockingbirds
	May 1949, orange blossom, Golden rod, Magnolia, Blue Bonnet
	February 1950, rooster, hens and chicks
	March 1950, chickens
	March 1953, southern state flowers; Cherokee Rose, Apple Blossom, iris and rhododendron
	November 1953, Turkey
	January 1954, geese and guinea
	June 1954, Peacock
	June 1956 Blossoms of Cotton, corn and tobacco
	July 1956 Ruby-throated Hummingbird and morning glories
Southern Accents	November 12, 1987, "The Southern Artist: Athos Menaboni"
Sports Afield	January 1951
	January 1955, Bobwhite
Sports Illustrated	November 15, 1954, Shoveller Duck
	October 10, 1955 Chukar Partridge

Notes

[1] Allan Bryant, "Menaboni Lives with the Birds He Paints," *Atlanta Journal and Constitution Magazine* (December 12, 1954): 12.

[2] Andrew Sparks, "Artist's Wife Finds Geese in the Bathtub—Eggs in the Chandelier," *Atlanta Journal and Constitution Magazine* (November 5, 1950).

[3] Taken from Sara's story "Athos Menaboni: The Man," November 1963.

[4] Laura C. Lieberman, "The Southern Artist, Athos Menaboni," *Southern Accents* (November/December 1987): 149.

[5] Athos and Sara Menaboni, *Menaboni's Birds* (Rinehart & Company, Inc. New York/Toronto, 1950) 60.

[6] Agnes Fahy, "Painting the Sky," *Atlanta Journal*, June 10, 1928.

[7] Charles Elliott, *Ichauway Plantation* (Robert W. Woodruff, 1974) 98.

[8] Robert Woodruff, was instrumental in securing Athos to execute this commission work. Innovative interior decorator Molly Aeck, wife of architect Richard Aeck, and best friend of Sara Menaboni, had envisioned and employed Athos to paint two glass panels some time before the Mirador Room's inception. The inspiration for painting glass panels was to enable a view of the magnificently trained and feathered dress worn by her client, Mrs. Howell, when presented in court in London while it hung majestically in the closet of this room she designed called the Persian Room.

[9] James C. Bryant, *The Mirador Room, Memories of an Era, 1939-1998* (Atlanta GA: Capital City Club) 11.

[10] Sara Menaboni to Mr. Frank H. Griggs, of Abreu and Robeson, *Journal/Callaway Gardens*, May 27, 1978.

[11] Allan Bryant, "Menaboni Lives with the Birds He Paints," *Atlanta Journal and Constitution Magazine* (December 12, 1954).

[12] Sara Menaboni to Betty Skiles, February 2, 1987, copy of letter in author's possession.

[13] Howard Pousner, "Portrait of a Nature Artist," *Atlanta Journal/Constitution*, December 23, 1984, 1J.

[14] Frank Daniel, "Blind Bird Homes True to Athos Menaboni," *Atlanta Journal*, December 28, 1962.

[15] Harry Phillips, "Memo from the publisher," *Sports Illustrated*, (November 8, 1954).